SPECIAL SERIES NO. 17   15 AUGUST 1943

GERMAN DOCTRINE
OF THE STABILIZED FRONT

PREPARED BY

MILITARY INTELLIGENCE DIVISION

WAR DEPARTAMENT • WASHINGTON, DC

Published by Books Express Publishing
Copyright © Books Express, 2011
ISBN 978-1-780390-77-2

Books Express publications are available from all good retail and online booksellers. For
publishing proposals and direct ordering please contact us at: info@books-express.com

The previous issues of *Special Series* are listed below. All of these issues have been classified as "restricted," with the exception of Nos. 12 and 13, which have been placed in a lower category, "not to be published," and No. 15, which is "confidential." [1]

1. *British Commandos* (9 August 1942).
2. *The German Armored Army* (10 August 1942).
3. *German Military Training* (17 September 1942).
4. *The German Motorized Infantry Regiment* (17 October 1942).
5. *The Development of German Defensive Tactics in Cyrenaica—1941* (16 October 1942).
6. *Artillery in the Desert* (25 November 1942).
7. *Enemy Air-Borne Forces* (2 December 1942).
8. *German Tactical Doctrine* (20 December 1942).
9. *The German Squad in Combat* (25 January 1943).
10. *German Antiaircraft Artillery* (8 February 1943).
11. *Morale-Building Activities in Foreign Armies* (15 March 1943).
12. *German Military Abbreviations* (12 April 1943).
13. *British Military Terminology* (15 May 1943).
14. *German Infantry Weapons* (25 May 1943).
15. *German Coastal Defenses* (15 June 1943).
16. *Enemy Capabilities for Chemical Warfare* (15 July 1943).

---

[1] One unnumbered issue, *German Military Symbols* (classified as "not to be published"), appeared in January 1943.

MILITARY INTELLIGENCE DIVISION
WAR DEPARTMENT
WASHINGTON 25, 15 AUGUST 1948

SPECIAL SERIES
No. 17
MID 461

NOTICE

1. Publication of *Special Series* is for the purpose of providing officers with reasonably confirmed information from official and other reliable sources.

2. In order to meet the specific request of appropriate headquarters, or in order to conserve shipping space, the distribution of any particular issue of *Special Series* may be modified from the standard. This issue, owing to its high classification, is being given a limited distribution. Distribution to air units is being made by the Assistant Chief of Air Staff, Intelligence, Army Air Forces.

3. Each command should circulate available copies among its officers. Reproduction within the military service is permitted provided (1) the source is stated, (2) the classification is not changed, and (3) the information is safeguarded. *Paragraphs 1 through 11 may be reproduced and disseminated as restricted matter.*

4. Readers are invited to comment on the use that they are making of this publication and to forward suggestions for future issues. Such correspondence may be addressed directly to the Dissemination Unit, Military Intelligence Division, War Department, Washington 25, D. C.

Other publications of the Military Intelligence Division include: *Tactical and Technical Trends* (biweekly); *Intelligence Bulletin* (monthly); *Military Reports on the United Nations* (monthly).

Requests for additional copies of publications of the Military Intelligence Division should be forwarded through channels for approval.

I

CONTENTS

IV CONTENTS

ILLUSTRATIONS

Section II. TACTICAL

---

1. ROLE OF TROOPS

a. Offensive Spirit

German doctrine holds that the infantry must be the deciding factor in combat within fortified zones, as well as in a war of movement. The tenacious resistance of the infantry under even the heaviest fire, and its fighting spirit in making counterattacks, are the measure of the strength of the defense. The decision is usually achieved on the ground between bunkers by the infantryman in hand-to-hand combat—with his rifle, bayonet, and hand grenade. No less determined must be the defense of any permanent installation, according to the German doctrine, which states that the main fortified position must be held against all attacks, and that each link in its works must be defended to the last bullet. An effort is made to imbue every German soldier with the will to destroy the attacker. The German soldier is also taught to continue to fight even though the tide of battle flows over and around him.

Permanent fortifications, the German soldier is told, must never be surrendered, even when all weapons are out of action through lack of ammunition or reduction of the position. The reason for this principle is that the perseverance of the garrison, even without active fighting, impedes the enemy's advance and facilitates the counterattack. Herein lies a basic difference between the German view of defensive fighting on perma-

FOREWORD

German policy has consistently emphasized the development of highly mobile armies, and Germany's military successes have been gained in wars of maneuver. During the past 25 years the German High Command has become thoroughly convinced of the soundness of the Schlieffen theories of movement, envelopment, and annihilation, especially since Germany's central location in Europe gives her the advantage of interior lines of communication—a decided strategic advantage in a war of maneuver. Indoctrined and trained in the Schlieffen theories, German armies were successful in the Franco-Prussian War, in World War I (until they became involved in trench warfare of attrition), and in the Polish, Norwegian, and western European campaigns of World War II.

However, Germany's central position ceases to be an advantage whenever her enemies can so combine that they engage her in a two-front war. Her transportation, manpower, and other resources are not sufficient to insure a decisive victory on two sides at once. In order to escape this prospect, the German ʒh Command reached the conclusion that at least ⌐⌐ one side Germany could and must secure herself with a great fortified system.

A doctrine of permanent fortifications, exhaustive in scope, was formulated under the title "The Stabilized Front" (*Die Ständige Front*). The classic concept of fortifications—isolated fortress cities and a line of fortified works—was abandoned as obsolete. The German High Command developed new principles in the light of modern warfare, weapons, and air power which called for the construction of permanent fortifications in systems of zones, organized in great depth. By "stabilized front" they meant not only the fixed positions which the field armies might be compelled to establish during a campaign, but also the deep zones of fortified works which would be constructed in peacetime. (See par. **8**, p. 24.)

The primary mission of the fortifications in the west was to serve at the proper time as the springboard for an attack; however, until that time came, they were to protect Germany's western flank while she waged offensive war in the east. Thus the West Wall was conceived as a great barrier against France and the Low Countries. But it is essential to realize that the conception of the West Wall, far from committing the German High Command to a passively defensive attitude, gave all the greater scope to the offensive character of its doctrine. The entire German Army, including the units assigned to the West Wall, was indoctrinated with the offensive spirit and thoroughly trained for a war of movement.

The role of fortifications in the German strategy was summarized in the following statement of General von Brauchitsch, then German Commander-in-Chief, in September 1939:

"The erection of the West Wall, the strongest fortification in the world, enabled us to destroy the Polish

Army in the shortest possible time without obliging us to split up the mass of our forces at various fronts, as was the case in 1914. Now that we have no enemy in the rear, we can calmly await the future development of events without encountering the danger of a two-front war."

This study does not propose to judge the soundness of the German concept of fortifications. It may be pointed out, however, that in formulating its doctrine, the German High Command did not foresee that the German West Wall and the great coastal defenses in the occupied countries would not protect vital war industries against massive and destructive attacks from the air. The aim of this study is to provide a digest of German principles of modern fortifications and the available information concerning the various lines of permanent and field fortifications which Germany has constructed within and outside her frontiers.

Part 1

GERMAN PRINCIPLES OF FORTIFICATIONS

Section I. STRATEGIC

The Germans regard economy of force as the fundamental rule to be observed in planning zones of permanent fortifications. Their aim is to achieve an effective defense with a minimum of manpower so that the bulk of the field armies will be left mobile and free for offensive action elsewhere. In other words, a very small portion of the nation's military strength or of its training effort is allocated specifically to the permanent defenses, and even the troops that are assigned to fortifications receive the same tactical training as the troops in the field armies.

A permanently fortified zone, as the Germans conceive it, must serve two purposes: primarily it is to be a base for offensive operations, and secondarily it is designed to protect some vital area or interest of the defender.

The value of such a zone depends upon the length and geographic nature of the national frontiers, the funds available for its construction, and the potential strength of the enemy. According to German doctrine, there is no real military value in a fortified zone which may be strategically outflanked; neither is there any reason for such fortifications when the opposing combination is either much weaker or much stronger than the defender. Likewise the economic cost of a fortification system must not be so great as to deprive the field armies of adequate funds for training and

2

equipment, but enough must be expended to make it as strong as necessary. The German doctrine also assumes that the natural progress of technology will produce weapons which will limit the value of any specific defenses to a term of years. Therefore, the Germans construct their fortifications to solve a definite existing strategic problem rather than to forestall the problems of the future.

For the purposes of strategic offense, the Germans place a fortified zone close enough to the border to serve as a basis of military operations against the neighboring nation. For the purposes of strategic defense, they construct it far enough back from the frontier to deprive an enemy attack of force before it can reach the main defenses. In either case, the fortified zone is generally located far enough inside the border to make it impossible for the enemy to bombard it with heavy batteries emplaced on his own soil. However, in exceptional cases—where, for instance, heavy industries must be protected—the Germans may build a defensive zone immediately adjoining the enemy border.

In a German fortified system the flanks are drawn back as far as possible, unless they can be rested on impregnable natural obstacles or on the frontiers of friendly countries which are capable of maintaining their neutrality.

When a German fortified zone lies along a river bank, the system includes a number of bridges and large bridgeheads, so that the defenders may carry out counterattacks. As always, German defensive doctrine is posited upon the principle that offensive action is ultimately the best protection.

The fortified zone as conceived by German theorists is designed to permit free lateral movement of troops, and to provide space and means for effective counter-attack. For the offensive, the Germans maintain, a zone of man-made fortifications has definite advantages over natural obstacles, such as mountain ranges or rivers, because a zone system permits field armies to debouch for an attack at any desired point or points. Likewise, field forces may retire more easily through a fortified zone.

Isolated fortifications like the fortress city, even those provided with all-around protection, are considered obsolete by the Germans, who have concluded that the civil population of a fortress city is a burden to the defenders, and, moreover, that such a city is vulnerable to incendiary air bombardment.

nent fortified fronts and of the defense in war of movement: in the latter the loss of an individual position is not considered critical.

Heavy infantry weapons and the artillery are the backbone of the German defense in a permanent position. During heavy and prolonged bombardment, the permanent installations, with their concrete and armor plate, protect the weapons and their crews, and keep the unengaged troops in fighting trim for the eventual counterattack. In this sense only, the Germans consider fortified zones tactically defensive in character. Individual bunkers may be taken by a determined attacker, but, because of their large number and dispersion, organized resistance by the remaining works can continue until mobile forces are brought up to eject the enemy.

b. Counterattack

The Germans consider it essential to make provision for small local infantry reserves in a fortified position. These reserves are protected by strong overhead cover and can be shifted rapidly by means of underground tunnels to the area where they are required for counterattack. As soon as the attacker has taken possession of any portion of the fortified zone, these reserves are sent into action in order to strike before the enemy can organize his gains. For the counterattack, the Germans claim the defender has the advantage of a coordinated and complete observation and communication system. In addition the defender brings his sheltered reserves into action in fresh condition, without the casualties that are suffered when they pass through artillery fire, and without the loss of time entailed in bringing reserves up from the rear.

The Germans attempt to provide against the failure of the local reserves to break up an attack by arranging for additional reserves to be brought up from the rear, either by underground tunnels or by camouflaged roads. Every effort is made to give these reserves artillery support and to acquaint them thoroughly with the terrain. Sector reserves and the units of the intermediate zone may begin the counterattack without specific orders. Units with security missions do not take part in the counterattack.

The Germans believe that the most favorable time for a large-scale counterattack is the moment when the enemy artillery and antitank weapons are advancing to new positions. Provided the situation permits, the afternoon is considered preferable to morning, because then, after the objective is reached, the regained terrain can be consolidated during the hours of darkness.

As a rule, the troops held in readiness for a general counterattack are employed as a unit. The Germans consider it advantageous to attach them to a division in line for the sake of the uniform conduct of battle. If the situation requires that parts of a division be detached for the support of other units, the Germans subordinate them to the commander of the corresponding battle sector.

Should the enemy succeed in penetrating the main fortified position at several points, the Germans prescribe that the other attacked positions must continue the battle without regard to the situation at the points of penetration. The enemy penetrations are dealt with by battle installations in the rear, protective flank installations, and heavy infantry weapons not otherwise employed, which direct their fire against the points of penetration and attempt to destroy the enemy before he consolidates his gains. The Germans constantly renew barrage fire of all weapons beyond the points of enemy penetration in order to delay the enemy and make it difficult for him to bring up additional troops. Isolated battle installations, for which the enemy is fighting in close combat, are brought under the controlled fire of neighboring light and heavy infantry weapons, and of light artillery. However, the heavy infantry guns are not employed in such a situation in order that crews within the friendly installations will not be endangered.

c. Relief

Another essential function of German reserves is regularly to relieve troops employed in a fortified zone in order that their fighting strength may be maintained or restored. Because of the special missions of permanent troops, their relief can be thoroughly prepared, and is carried out without interrupting the continuity of the defense. The length of relief depends on the condition of the men as well as on the strength of available forces. The relief is effected in such a manner that the relieving units arrive after dark, and in any sector which is subject to ground observation the relieved units move out before daybreak. Advance detachments prepare the relief; guides and orientation detachments direct the relieving units. Complete readiness for defense is maintained, and the usual combat activities are continued at all times during these relieving operations.

2. PERMANENT AND FIELD FORTIFICATIONS

a. Comparison of Permanent and Field Works

The Germans realize that while permanent fortifications conserve manpower, they require a great deal of money and labor prior to hostilities. Field fortifications cost much less in labor and money but require strong forces and great courage for their defense. The Germans also realize that both modern tanks and high-angle heavy artillery weapons are so mobile that the attacker can always bring them within range of any defensive zone. The fire of these weapons, as well as air bombardment, is effective against field fortifications, but it is not so serious against permanent defensive works. The ideal solution of the problem in a modern defensive system, the Germans conclude, is to lay out both permanent and field fortifications so that they complement each other and take full advantage of the terrain.

Another German principle is that the weakest terrain should be provided with the strongest and most numerous permanent defensive works, organized in great depth, but only after the relative defense effectiveness of the terrain and of permanent fortifications has been carefully judged. The defended zone is everywhere made as strong as the available resources permit, and no terrain is left entirely without the protective fire of some permanent defensive works.

b. Characteristics of Individual Works

The Germans have recognized the rule that the defensive strength of a fortification system depends upon the ability of individual works to deliver continuous short-range flanking and supporting fire from automatic weapons, and to afford moral and physical protection, relief, and unlimited ammunition supply for the defending crews. The works are placed far enough apart so that enemy artillery fire that misses one installation will not hit the others. Also, they are so placed that all the terrain is effectively covered by observation and fire. In the general organization of a position, the Germans endeavor to make it difficult for the enemy to discover the vital centers of resistance so that he may be kept in doubt as to where he should employ his heavy indirect fire.

Widely distributed works are generally joined by connecting trenches to form defensive systems. Fortifications are constructed for all-around defense of platoon or company defense areas; they may be combined into closely organized battalion defense areas or echeloned in width and depth. The strength, size, garrison, armament, and equipment of such works depend upon the mission of the fortifications. They are so located as to permit a system of zone defenses. Fire from such positions, the Germans believe, is especially effective because even under enemy bombardment exact aim and rigid fire control can be maintained. Large isolated permanent fortifications unsupported by the fire of other fortifications are considered obsolete by the Germans.

Because of the relative dispersion of the works and of the thoroughness of the antiaircraft defenses, the Germans consider air bombardment an uneconomical means of destroying a modern fortification system. Therefore, they employ a greater proportion of the defending air forces in general support, as well as in local support of large counterattacks.

Where decisive resistance is to be maintained, the Germans design concrete and steel works strong enough to provide moral and physical protection against the enemy's heaviest indirect fire. Careful study is made of enemy artillery—its power, range and mobility—and special provision is made in those areas which can be reached by long-range guns. The Germans believe that the thickness of concrete covering necessary to withstand effective artillery fire is approximately ten times the maximum caliber of the artillery that may fire on it. When the German High Command has decided that a permanent fortification is required, it specifies that it should be built according to these basic requirements.

Infantry weapons only are generally emplaced in permanent works. Artillery and other supporting arms are placed mainly in open positions, with their normal field protection, in order to retain mobility. At critical points where continuous fire is essential, some artillery may be permanently emplaced.

Concrete bunkers are generally used for flanking fire in positions which are protected from direct observation by the enemy. Steel turrets are used on all works which fire frontally and which consequently are constructed with low silhouettes for good concealment; they are also considered essential for flanking fire in flat terrain.

c. Field Fortifications

German permanent works are supplemented extensively by field fortifications and alternate weapon emplacements whose fire missions include protection of sally ports, communication routes, and defiladed areas. The field fortifications also allow crews to continue the fight when their permanent positions have been neutralized, and provide firing positions for reserves in the counterattack.

According to German doctrine, field fortifications are constructed in time of tension or war to reinforce stabilized fronts. The construction of these works is carried out according to plans prepared in peacetime by construction units or by troop units assigned to the fortifications. Available equipment and tools and, to some extent, building materials prepared in peacetime are used for this purpose. With a conflict imminent or already started, construction embraces the works listed below, the number and scope in each sector being dependent on the strength of fortifications that were completed in peacetime:

(1) Obstacles in the outpost area.

(2) Reinforcement of the obstacles in the advanced position and in the main battle position.

(3) Open emplacements for light and heavy infantry weapons in the terrain between permanent installations, and in the depth of the main battle position.

(4) Splinterproof dugouts in the vicinity of the emplacements.

(5) Observation posts, artillery emplacements, and cover for the crews.

(6) Command posts and dugouts of all kinds.

(7) Trenches of all kinds—shallow and normal communication trenches, fire trenches, approach trenches, and telephone wire trenches.

(8) Dummy installations and camouflage.

(9) Deep shelters in the rear sector of the main battle position, and also behind the battle position, if the terrain is suitable.

(10) Flanking obstacles and rear positions.

The value of field fortifications lies, according to German principles, in their small size, their great number, and their slight camouflage requirements. They compel the enemy to disperse his fire.

Temporary emplacements for heavy infantry weapons and artillery are employed to engage the approaching enemy in the advanced and outpost positions without betraying the location of the permanent installations. Temporary positions may also be used as alternate positions. The construction, as well as the maintenance and repair of field fortifications, is continued by the troops during combat. Dugouts affording more protection than splinterproof shelters are constructed for the troops.

d. Depth

German fortified zones are laid out deep enough to compel the attacking artillery and its ammunition service to change positions during the attack. The aim is to deprive the attacker of surprise effect, and to cause him to lose valuable time, which may be used by the defender in organizing a counterattack.

If a limitation of funds does not permit the construction of a zone of uniform density that would fulfill the requirement of depth, the Germans construct two parallel fortified belts of maximum strength, separated by that distance which will insure maximum disorganization and embarrassment to the attacking artillery. The intermediate terrain between these belts is provided with permanent works, which, though lacking density, are so sited that progress through them will be slow and difficult. Field fortifications are also constructed in the intermediate area, and from them machine guns, antitank guns, and other infantry weapons supplement and reinforce the defensive fire. Obstacles of all types are employed extensively throughout a zone to delay and force the enemy to advance into a particular area that is best suited for defense.

The outpost area, which includes fortifications of all possible types, is also calculated to give depth to a German fortified zone, and to help in absorbing any surprise attack that is directed against the main position. The mission of troops in this area is to prevent the enemy from laying observed artillery fire on the main battle position, to delay his approach, and to inflict casualties. Part of the mission of German combat outposts is to prevent the enemy from conducting terrain and combat reconnaissance toward the main fortified belt.

3. FIRE CONTROL

a. Gapless Firing Chart

The basis for the defense of a main position in a German fortified system is the gapless firing chart. The effective field of fire of the heavy infantry weapons from their fixed positions is determined by the limits of their loopholes. Infantry weapons emplaced in field fortifications supplement this fire. The heavy infantry weapons also participate in harassing, destructive, and barrage fire according to their effective range, but their chief mission is defense against assault. If the enemy succeeds in driving back the advanced forces and the combat outposts and begins to attack the fortifications, the Germans open from the fixed positions a defensive fire based on data that was previously prepared and included in the chart.

The firing chart regulates the coordination and the distribution of fire of the weapons installed in the permanent and the field fortifications so that all areas in which an attack may occur can be controlled. Because loophole fire from permanent fortification is limited on the flanks, the Germans provide support, especially with machine guns, from field works.

The position from which enemy weapons may open fire against loopholes is estimated in advance by the troops manning each loophole. Mines may also be laid at appropriate points. The German firing chart is designed to guarantee a continuous belt of fire, even if individual fortifications are put out of action. Regimental commanders are responsible for coordinating firing charts at the boundaries of the battalion sectors.

The German firing chart is based on a battalion sector, and sometimes separate charts may be set up for a fortification or a group of fortifications.

b. Distribution and Control of Fire

The decision to open fire is made by the battalion commander, or by the commander of a fortification or group of fortifications. The subordinate commanders of works may open fire independently as soon as they have received the "fire at will" order from the battalion or fortification commander. To stop the enemy early, the Germans prescribe that fire must be opened at long range in accordance with the data in the firing chart.

The weapons of a German permanent fortification do not remain inactive, not even while being fired on. They endeavor to delay the approach of the attacker immediately, and especially to prevent individual enemy guns from being emplaced. The weapons of the concrete works first engage from the flanks the most dangerous targets which appear in their combat sector, and, therefore, such works are provided with frontal protection by permanent and field positions. Targets in the sectors of other works are engaged only on the order of a superior commander, even though the targets seem worth-while.

Combat sectors are subdivided into gun sectors because in the six-loophole armored turrets of German fortifications the machine guns fire, as a rule, on separate targets. Because of the position of the loopholes, combined fire from both machine guns can be employed only in exceptional cases, and then only at medium and long ranges. The fire is combined if the target is in range of both guns, and if a decisive effect can be attained.

By frequent and rapid change of targets, pillboxes fire on many targets in a short time, thus utilizing thoroughly the fire effect of the weapons. If a change of target necessitates a change of loopholes, the shift is accomplished by the machine guns successively, to avoid interruption of fire effect. Since mortars supplement the defensive fire of the machine guns, especially in broken terrain, close cooperation with the machine guns in the bunkers is sought. Mortars installed in the field support the fire of the other heavy infantry weapons and the artillery in places where the effect of the latter two weapons is not sufficient.

Infantry guns open fire as soon and as heavily as possible. Their chief mission is to engage troublesome targets which cannot be reached by other weapons. In employing weapons emplaced in bunkers, the Germans open fire as soon as the enemy reaches the effective range of their flanking weapons. If a bunker is put out of action, the neighboring works take over its combat sector. By flanking fire they attempt to prevent any enemy penetration through the resulting gap, insofar as this is permitted by the effective range of their weapons and the necessity for defending their own frontal sector. German troops are taught that when a position is lost, flanking fire from neighboring positions may be decisive in repelling an enemy penetration.

c. Control of Machine-Gun Fire

Machine guns are the chief source of German infantry fire from combat positions. The commanders of positions direct the machine-gun fire in accordance with the combat orders for their position, and, as a rule, order direct laying on the strength of their own observations.

Targets to be engaged by machine guns in pillboxes are assigned by fortification commanders in accordance with the data furnished by observers in turrets or armored observation towers. If the designated targets cannot be seen from bunkers, or if the targets are screened by smoke, the observers take over control of fire also.

In six-loophole armored turrets, the gunners usually engage the target independently after the fire order has been given. Turret commanders supervise simultaneously the fire of both turret machine guns and observe continuously the entire combat sector.

4. ANTITANK DEFENSE

A German defensive zone is protected against tank attacks by natural or artificial obstacles which are covered by suitable antitank weapons of all kinds. In the outpost area, strong mobile antitank units are attached to the forces employed in the outpost area to deal with enemy armored forces.

The chief mission of stationary antitank guns of all calibers and of certain specially designated artillery in a German fortified zone is to destroy the medium or heavy infantry support tanks, which might attack the loopholes of works in a main fortified position.

Should the enemy succeed in penetrating the main fortified position, the Germans prepare for the appearance of strong tank forces in an afterthrust to widen the point of penetration. Should enemy tank forces attempt a further penetration of the main position, mobile reserves of antitank units, mobile engineer forces held in readiness with Tellermines, and mobile reserves of heavy and light antiaircraft guns of the Air Force commander are employed to engage them. In some situations the Germans combine their divisional antitank battalions for uniform employment by the corps or higher command. In cases of immediate danger, the Germans require their antiaircraft artillery to give priority to defense against tank attacks rather than air attacks.

If reinforcement of fixed antitank defenses in a fortified zone becomes necessary, the infantry antitank company is employed for this purpose in field positions among the fortified works. The antitank company in such a case is subordinated to the sector commander, as are the fixed antitank defenses. However, the use of infantry antitank units for the relief of permanent antitank defenses is considered exceptional. The German infantry company provides the necessary depth for the antitank defense of the regimental sector. Only in exceptional cases, as in terrain absolutely secure against tank attack and well protected by effective obstacles and a sufficient number of antitank guns, is the infantry antitank company to be used as a mobile reserve. Its disposition depends on its mobility and its ability to maneuver across country.

The fixed antitank weapons are manned and relieved by fortification antitank units.

Infantry antitank units using embrasured antitank emplacements, antitank guns employed in intermediate terrain, and antitank riflemen engage principally light and medium tanks. Heavy tanks are engaged by special antitank weapons, supported by artillery and combat engineers. Machine guns emplaced in the fortifications normally fire on enemy infantry, and also fire at the observation slits of the tanks.

5. ARTILLERY

German artillery in a fortified zone consists of position artillery, which is stationary or of limited maneuverability, mobile divisional artillery, and army artillery, used for reinforcement. The bulk of the defending artillery is highly mobile in order that it may be employed for mass effect at the point where the enemy attempts a decisive attack. Artillery positions are prepared in the outpost area throughout the fortified zone, and in rear of this zone for the maximum number of artillery batteries required. These positions are laid out as much as possible near defiladed routes of approach. The positions also include protection for men and ammunition, and have an underground communication system to previously established observation posts which are usually located in armored turrets.

In the initial stage of combat the bulk of the light and medium defending artillery is held in the advanced positions for counterbattery and counterpreparation missions. If their defending artillery is forced to displace by an attack that reaches the fortified zone, the Germans concentrate maximum fire on the enemy infantry in order effectively to prepare a counterattack. For this purpose, a certain number of batteries in the fortified zone are emplaced behind protection that can withstand the heaviest enemy artillery fire. Such batteries are permanently emplaced.

In case the counterattack fails and the defending divisional artillery is forced to evacuate the forward areas of the fortified zone, the Germans give this artillery the extremely important mission of concentrating its entire fire on the enemy infantry.

The Germans have laid down the doctrine that the closest liaison between artillery and infantry and the local collaboration of artillery with all other branches of the service are decisive factors in the conduct of artillery combat and in the outcome of the defense. They prescribe that this cooperation must be established and maintained in every way. German artillery is trained to take the following deceptive measures:

a. Repeated changes of positions between missions.

b. Restricted activity from the firing position chosen for the main decisive battle.

c. Individual missions and harassing fire are carried out principally by changing the range and by roving batteries.

d. A number of silent batteries are held in reserve so as to be available for special missions during enemy attack.

6. OBSERVATION, RECONNAISSANCE, AND REPORTS

Constant observation of the terrain from all fortifications, before the approach of the enemy and during the attack, is regarded as of the utmost importance by the Germans. Observation is not permitted to lapse during pauses in fire, particularly during darkness or fog. In works which have no field optical instruments, observation is maintained through loopholes. In bunkers, armored turrets, and observation posts, standard fixed optical instruments are used for this purpose. Sufficient instruments are issued to permit extensive, gapless, and safe observation of the entire combat terrain.

All useful observations are reported at once to higher headquarters and passed along to the commanders of other fortifications. Furthermore, at times designated by higher headquarters, fortification commanders make brief daily reports, including—

a. Conclusions drawn from observations of the enemy.

b. Engagements.

c. Combat strength and losses.

d. Condition of fortifications, weapons, and instruments.

e. Requisitions for replacements and supplies.

The chief mission of German army reconnaissance aircraft attached to the corps general staff is to secure advance information about enemy preparations for attack. In large-scale fighting, the Germans use reconnaissance planes to clarify their own situation also. During quiet periods, such aircraft superintend the camouflaging of finished combat installations, as well as those under construction.

Individual aircraft may be attached to German divisions for the purpose of aiding the artillery to adjust on rear enemy areas.

7. COMMUNICATION AND CONTROL

All commanders in a German fortified zone are kept fully informed at all times of the actual situation within their area of command. In an effort to insure a continual flow of information, the Germans try to maintain a communication system that will function without fail under the heaviest possible fire of the enemy. Usually a double cable system, buried beyond the effect of the heaviest air bombs and artillery shells, is employed in a stabilized position.

For the purpose of efficient command control, neighboring bunkers or turrets are united into a group or fortress by underground tunnels. In this way, the German Army tries to assure not only greater tactical control, but also greater tactical strength. Each fortress forms a battalion defense area in which the individual forts are capable of mutual support. The bunkers with maximum observation and fire power are the focal points of the new system, and are provided with complete flanking fire from fortifications within the group or from additional bunkers constructed for this purpose. Wire obstacles covered by this flanking fire are camouflaged as carefully as possible in order not to betray to the attacker the positions of flanking bunkers and the battalion defense areas.

Section III. EXCERPTS FROM "THE STABILIZED FRONT"

8. GENERAL

The Germans teach that defensive combat on a stabilized front is conducted generally according to the same principles as the defense in a war of movement, the chief consideration being the tactical organization of the defensive fires and forces. The stabilized front consists of an outpost area and one or more continuous main areas of fortifications in depth. Within the meaning of the term "stabilized front," the Germans include zones of permanent fortifications constructed in peacetime, like the West Wall, and fixed positions assumed through necessity during the course of a campaign.

The extent of construction in a German stabilized position depends upon the operational importance of the entire front and the tactical importance of the individual sector, the terrain, and the mission of the fortifications. The maintenance and repair of all works during battle are the responsibility of the crews and troops employed in them.

The subject of the fixed position is covered in "The Stabilized Front" (*Die Ständige Front*) which is the designation of German Field Manual 89, printed in tentative form by the Government Printing Office in Berlin in 1939.

Much of the material contained in the manual is obsolete, the Germans having adapted their doctrine to the tactical lessons learned on the battlefield since 1939. However, certain revealing principles of fortification have been digested and included in this study. In this section are quoted parts which are applicable to a study of German zone fortifications.

9. OUTLINE OF BATTLE ORDER FOR BATTALION SECTOR

a. Evaluation of Terrain for Enemy Attack

(1) Disposition of troops.
(2) Observation posts.
(3) Weapons for loophole firing.
(4) Terrain secure from tank attack.
(5) Points of main effort of hostile attack.

b. Firing Chart

(1) Section of 1/25,000 map with range sketch.
(2) Orders for individual weapons.

(*a*) Sectors of observation and effectiveness for long-range fire—Opening of fire—Harassing fire.

(*b*) Sectors of observation and effectiveness for medium and close range—Opening of fire.

(*c*) Preparation for fire concentrations upon critical terrain—Destructive fire.

(*d*) Regulation of fire of silent weapons as to time and sector.

(*e*) Time and space specifications for barrage—Employment of ammunition—Justification and means for opening barrage.

(*f*) Defensive fires on enemy penetrations—Support of counterattacks.

(*g*) Artillery observation posts—Communications with artillery.

(*h*) Line before which an enemy tank attack must be caused to fail.

c. Main Line of Resistance

(1) Sector boundaries.

(2) Type and location of obstacles.

d. Combat Outposts

(1) Mission and strength.

(2) Destination and route.

(3) Authority to issue orders.

e. Reserves

(1) Possible employment and routes.

(2) Time schedule.

f. Command Posts in Sector

g. Channel of Communication

Sketch supplied by commander.

h. Map—Composition of Armed Works in Each Company Sector

(1) Loophole emplacements.

(*a*) Machine guns.

(*b*) Antitank guns.

(2) Bunkers.

(*a*) Machine guns.

(*b*) Antitank guns.

(3) Armored loophole turrets—Type and number of loopholes.

(4) Armored mortar turrets.
(5) Observation installations.
(*a*) Map—Location and capacity of dugouts.
(*b*) Supplementary fixed weapons.

i. Ammunition Supply

Types and amounts.

j. Additional Garrison for Positions

(1) Strength.
(2) Weapons.

k. Emergency Alarms

(1) Alert.
(2) Gas.
(3) Air raid.

l. Administration

Rations.

m. Medical Facilities

10. OUTLINE OF COMBAT INSTRUCTIONS FOR AN INDIVIDUAL WORK

Combat instruction for _____ of the _____ Company.

a. Panoramic Sketch

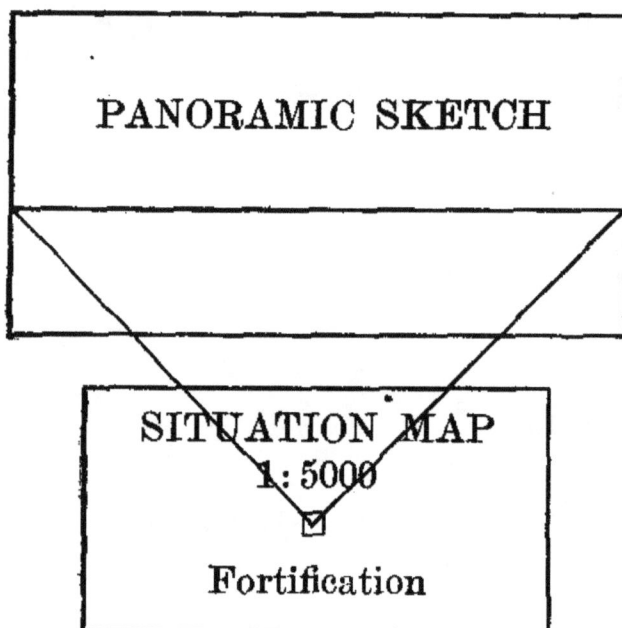

(On the panoramic sketch are entered the important terrain features and aiming points in the combat sector of the fortification. Each feature and point are given a designation.).

b. Combat Order

(1) Individual weapons in the fortification.
(2) Outer defense of the fortification.
(3) Troops occupying intermediate terrain.
(4) Execution of counterattacks.
(5) Withdrawal of combat posts.
(6) Scouts between the works.
(7) Type of fortification and adjacent works.
(8) Nearest commander.

(9) Fortification cable net.
(10) Channels of communication.
(11) Distribution of garrison.
(12) Observation posts.
(13) Supply.
(14) Emergency regulations.

c. Range Card

Aiming point	Range	Grad-uated ring (traverse)	Spirit level (eleva-tion)	Traversing stop		Search-ing fire	Remarks
				Right	Left		
•	•	•	•	•	•	•	•

d. Property List

(1) Fixed weapons.
(2) Ammunition supply and replenishment.
(3) Light and signal equipment.
(4) Emplacement equipment.
(5) Reserve rations.

11. SIGNAL COMMUNICATIONS

a. General

A dependable system of signal communications is of decisive importance for combat on a permanent front. Effective leadership would be impossible without it, and besides, it serves to strengthen the combat morale of personnel in the organized positions.

Before taking any tactical measures whatever, leadership must have the assurance that all signal communications are effectively established. As far as possible, changes in troop dispositions should not be made until the necessary changes in signal communications have also been made.

b. Duties of Staff Signal Officer

The army signal officer, on the basis of instructions received from the signal officer of the army group command, issues directions for the use of the facilities of the German Postal Service throughout the army area, in addition to supplying signal building material and equipment, and exercising control over further development of the signal network in the fortified positions. The army signal officer, in cooperation with the army quartermaster, likewise takes responsibility in advance for keeping communication equipment and spare parts for troops and fortifications at the army communication dump and in storage depots. He will also be responsible for delivering the equipment to the various organizations.

The corps general staff is responsible for the communication net in organized positions throughout the corps area. Special instructions concerning signal communications will be required when there is a change of sectors, when a new unit is brought into the position, and when communications between divisions are needed across sector boundaries.

The following are placed under the army communication officer:

(1) The army corps communication battalion (the army corps communication officer is the commanding officer of this battalion), and the fortification's com-

EXCERPTS FROM "THE STABILIZED FRONT"

munication staff, as well as attached platoons and details.

(2) The communication officer of the fortification's pioneer (engineer) staff (it is his duty to provide and maintain technical equipment for communications within permanent fortifications, and also to cooperate in the construction of buildings required for communications, such as blinker signal posts).

(3) The division communication officer (he is responsible for the communications net within the area assigned to the division; it is his duty to keep the corps signal officer currently informed on the state of maintenance and changes in the permanent net of the area).

On a stabilized front uniformity is absolutely essential in managing the net of communications throughout the division, even within the subordinate units. The communication officers of the individual units must cooperate with the division staff communication officer.

Staff and unit signal officers must familiarize themselves with the most important communication channels overlapping the neighboring sectors.

c. Fixed Communications on a Permanent Front

Fixed wire communication channels constitute the basis of signal communications on a permanent front. As compared with lines established to meet field conditions, these permanent lines are considerably better protected from enemy fire and interception, and they assure the transmission of orders between the fortifications and areas close to the rear.

As a safeguard against enemy action, all of the most important telephone communications should be duplicated. Advanced positions, advanced observation posts, and combat outposts in permanently organized fortifications are as a rule connected by ground cable with the net of the battle position. Defense works, heavy infantry weapons, and batteries in the advanced area will have to rely on signal communications equipment in the possession of the troops themselves, or upon the telephone net of the German Postal Service.

To facilitate the finding of the buried ground cable, a weather-resisting, orange-colored recognition band 2 centimeters (eight-tenths of an inch) in width is placed above the cable at a depth of about 0.40 meter (1 foot 4 inches). Proceed carefully when digging! The trace of the cable is indicated on the ground by stones used as cable markers.

d. Utilization of German Postal Service

The instructions in this paragraph apply not only to the German Postal Service net, but also to privately established telephone nets such as mine and forest systems. Decisions concerning utilization of the German Postal Service net are made by the army signal officer. The signal officer of the corps staff applies to him for connections for long distance and local wires, for the corps as a whole and also for the individual divisions.

e. Artillery Net

The most important lines are those connecting observation posts with firing positions and alternate firing positions, and those connecting the infantry with the artillery. Battalion command posts are connected by telephone lines with all observation posts of their sector, with the command posts of neighboring battalions, and with the higher artillery headquarters.

f. Sound-ranging Net

Sound-ranging nets are established by means of special cables which may not be used for purposes of conversation. Each observation post is linked with its plotting station by a telephone line for its exclusive use, and each sound-ranging station is connected with its plotting station by means of an exclusive sound-ranging wire. Each plotting station will require at least two telephone lines to link it with the observation battalion.

g. Flash-ranging Net

There is no necessity of keeping this net in special cables. Otherwise, the structure of this net corresponds to that of the sound-ranging net; flash-ranging connections constitute, therefore, part of the general net.

h. Infantry Net

There are direct lines connecting the division command post with each infantry regiment. The rear tie line is located at about the same depth as the infantry regimental command posts. It is used especially to maintain connections with the artillery, and to link infantry regimental command posts with one another. The rearward net is screened at approximately the depth of the infantry regimental command posts.

There are, in addition, special lines to the battalion command posts. The frontward tie line is located approximately at the depth of the battalion command posts. It is used for connections between the battalions, between infantry and artillery, and among different artillery organizations.

Each company commander is linked by telephone connections with his platoon commander, and the platoon and section commanders in turn are given a connection with their command posts. As a rule, the various command posts are linked together by groups. Party lines are most commonly used for these connections.

i. Duplication of Communications

The following can be used to duplicate parts of the signal nets:

      (1) Radio.
      (2) Heliograph.
      (3) Blinker apparatus.
      (4) Ground telegraph equipment.
      (5) Illuminants and signaling devices.
      (6) Messenger dogs.
      (7) Carrier pigeons.

j. Ground Telegraph Equipment

With the aid of this equipment it is possible to maintain communication over cables that have been severed by artillery fire. But since it affords no security against interception, this equipment has to be used very carefully. For that reason ground telegraph may not be used without the consent of the battalion commander. Report of its use should be made promptly to the division signal communication officer.

k. Illuminants and Signaling Devices

Organized battle positions are at present equipped not only with the army's usual illuminants and signaling devices, but also with a special emergency signal to be used by the garrison only in case of distress (this emergency signal equipment is in the course of development).

l. Messenger Dogs and Carrier Pigeons

The following principles apply to the use of messenger dogs and carrier pigeons:

(1) Messenger dogs are to be provided for areas in front of the regimental command posts. They are assigned to scout squads on reconnaissance duty. The messenger dogs may also be used on clearly visible terrain, on terrain that is difficult to cross or that is exposed to strong enemy fire, or under circumstances where alternate means of communication are not suitable. Depending on their memory for places, messenger dogs can be used for distances up to 1.5 kilometers (nine-tenths of a mile) and on artificial trails for distances up to 3 kilometers ($1\%_{10}$ miles).

(2) Messenger pigeons from permanent pigeon posts will be assigned to the various fortifications, shelters, and combat outposts, and possibly also to the platoon assigned to reconnaissance of enemy signal communications; or else they are turned over to scout squads for use on their missions. The pigeons are

released in flights of 2 or 4. A messenger pigeon post has about 300 pigeons. Of this number, up to 10 pigeons are to be left at each shelter and about 30 at each fortification.

(3) Telephone communication must be assured between the permanent carrier pigeon posts and the division command posts. Reports turned in at the division command post are passed on from there to the various duty stations concerned.

m. Transfer of Nets to Relief Units

When a relieving unit moves into the position, the new signal units should establish advance detachments at least 24 hours ahead of time. The signal personnel to be relieved should not be taken out until the new personnel have adapted themselves to the new position. Documents pertaining to radio operation and codes (including code names for telephone and blinker communication) should be taken over unchanged by the newly arrived troops to conceal the fact that there has been a relief. Change of personnel and of radio and code instructions must never be effected at the same time.

n. Maintaining Communications While Changing Sectors

Staff and unit communication officers, as well as permanently assigned signal personnel, must keep informed about the signal situation in the neighboring sectors in order to make it possible at any time to change sector limits without disrupting communications. Each unit concerned should place at the disposal of its neighbors a record of its own signal system. The circuit sketches of each unit must show connections across sector boundaries.

In some circumstances it may be advisable, for regiments transferred from their own to neighboring divisions, to depend temporarily on the connections of their former headquarters.

Connections that are not actually required for combat purposes should be dispensed with. Emphasis should be placed on the establishment of continuous transverse connections and on the linking of combat posts, the principal observation posts, and the battery firing positions.

o. Supplementing a Permanent Cable Net

In view of the danger of interception and the need for repairs, the use of field service lines to supplement the net of the permanent position should be kept at a minimum. Simplicity of arrangement is a requirement in adding these supplementary lines. Every precaution must be taken to insure that the net can be kept functioning by available personnel under heavy fire. Lines constructed by unit signal personnel must be checked by the division signal communication officer.

p. Maintenance and Repair

In the course of a defensive battle, it will not always be possible to keep all lines in order. In that event all available signal personnel will be used to reestablish the most important lines, giving up those lines which can be spared. Precedence must be given to maintenance of transverse connections and of the most important of the lines extending toward the front, such as those to command posts and observation posts.

q. Signal Intelligence Platoons

Signal intelligence platoons or platoons assigned to reconnoiter enemy signal communications should be employed according to tactical points of view. They should also be continuously informed and kept under continuous guidance. Furthermore, they should be furnished with information obtained by other reconnaissance units. Intelligence platoon leaders must continually endeavor to improve the training of their noncommissioned officers and men and to impart their experience to them. They should point out that their missions are of great importance even though the results attained may be slight.

The platoons covering enemy signal communications will receive, from the listening company in whose area they are located, directions to guide them in their reconnaissance work. The listening company will also report to the platoon the results of its reconnaissance of the division zone to which the platoon belongs.

Details ascertained by reconnaissance should be kept on file as permanent records, both in sketches and on index cards. Results can, as a rule, be obtained only from a comparative study of the details. Information should be exchanged with other types of reconnaissance units, such as the observation battalion. It is useful to exchange with neighboring divisions the results of reconnaissance covering enemy communications and the experience acquired. It is the duty of the army staff communication officer to assure cooperation between the listening companies and the reconnaissance platoons.

Important information, such as the appearance of tanks and other new units, relief of units, preparation of missions, and the effect of fire directed against the enemy, must be relayed at once to the nearest troops and to the division. The results obtained by reconnaissance platoons covering enemy communications should also be sent to the listening company. Steps must be taken to assure prompt and reliable transmission of information. Messenger pigeons are among the means of communication suited for this purpose. When messages are of great importance, several pigeons should be dispatched with the same message.

r. Radio Intelligence

It is the duty of radio intelligence troops to monitor radio communications of advanced enemy units. Enemy radio communication from division headquarters to the rear and radio communication between planes are monitored by fixed listening posts, listening companies, and listening posts of the air forces.

The range of enemy apparatus whose messages are to be intercepted is in many instances not in excess of a few kilometers. For that reason radio intelligence detachments must be placed well forward.

s. Wire Communication Intelligence

Valuable information may also be obtained by wire communication intelligence even though the results seem trifling. It is possible suddenly to intercept important information. The chances are especially good if the enemy's loop circuits have been damaged by cannon fire.

Where there is a lack of permanent signal installations, the newly arrived units themselves must set up temporary telephone interception posts. Dugouts of permanent construction are well adapted for use as telephone interception posts. If mines are embedded in the areas chosen for telephone interception installations, the lines should be placed in passages that are free of mines, so as to make it possible to provide for upkeep and repairs without danger. The closest cooperation with the local engineer commander is absolutely essential.

f. Protection against Interception

In view of the fact that signal installations on a stabilized front are fixed, there is a danger of their being tapped. All possible measures must be taken, therefore, to prevent the enemy from enjoying the advantage of effective reconnaissance of communications.

In the event that the enemy makes a breakthrough, lines leading in the direction of the enemy should be disconnected. When the advanced position is abandoned, lines leading into it should also be cut off. Similarly, when the enemy has broken into the main battle position, lines leading to works which are unmistakably held by the enemy should be disconnected.

Part 2

GERMAN FORTIFIED SYSTEMS

41

Section IV. INTERIOR AND COASTAL DEFENSES

12. GENERAL

Germany possesses elaborate fortifications on her own coasts and the coast lines of occupied countries, as well as in the interior and on land frontiers in regions where fortifications have offensive or defensive value. The sea frontier fortifications extend from Memel to Emden on the coast of Germany proper, and from Emden along the occupied coasts of the Netherlands, Belgium, and France to the Spanish border. The general location of the principal land and coastal fortification systems in western and eastern Europe are shown on the map, figure 1 (facing p. 142).

13. ORGANIZATION OF COASTAL DEFENSES

The coastal installations are Germany's first line of defense against invasion. The original German coastal fortifications were constructed, manned, and defended by the Navy in conjunction with the Air Force. However, new fortifications and improvements of old defenses on the German and the conquered coasts have been added since 1940 under the direction of the Army. In the absence of information to the contrary, it is presumed that the original naval fortifications on Germany's own coast line are still serviceable and probably greatly reinforced. They are administered by two naval territorial commands, the "North Sea Station" and the "Baltic Station." Under the commanding admiral of each station is a subordinate admiral, known as the "second admiral," in direct charge of the fortifications.

Germany's coastal defenses begin with obstructions in the water and extend inland, their strength and depth depending on the suitability of the beaches for hostile landings, the natural defensive strength of the terrain, and the strategic value of the portion of coast line concerned. In many cases the defenses reach depths of 35 miles from the coast. Many concrete emplacements, shelters, and other installations have been built along the possible landing beaches and around important ports; and the former French, Belgian, and Dutch defenses have been integrated into the German fortified system. Other installations, which the Germans have been busy constructing or improving for more than 3 years, are long-range fixed and railway guns, mobile coast-defense batteries, elaborate anti-aircraft emplacements, prepared positions for holding forces at all vulnerable points, and extensive water and beach obstacles.

For a detailed study of the types of installations on the occupied coasts of Europe, see "German Coastal Defenses," *Special Series*, No. 15 (15 June 1943).

In the German coastal defenses in France, Belgium, and the Netherlands, the smallest self-contained unit of the infantry positions is the shell-proof "defense post" (*Widerstandsnest*), which normally includes machine guns and occasionally antitank or infantry guns, and is held by a group of less than a platoon. A number of such defense posts, adapted to the terrain and affording mutual support, make up the familiar German "strongpoint" (*Stützpunkt*). Each strongpoint has all-around protection by fire, wire, and mines, and is provisioned to hold out for weeks if isolated. The coastal strongpoints are manned by units of company or larger size, and their armament includes the heavier infantry weapons. There are also naval, Air Force, and artillery stongpoints, which are usually centered on antiaircraft batteries or signal installations. Strongpoints are further combined into powerful fortified groups (*Stützpunktgruppen*), and in such combinations the groups include underground or sunken communications for the defense of particularly vital sectors. Such strongpoints include antiaircraft guns and heavy antitank guns, in addition to other weapons. Finally the defenses are organized into divisional coastal sectors (*Küstenverteidigungsabschnitte*).

14. WESTERN INTERIOR DEFENSES

a. From the Coast to the Maginot Line

Reports of German fortifications in the area between the Atlantic coast and the German frontier do not fully agree upon their nature and extent. However, it is certain that the Germans have taken advantage of the succession of excellent natural barriers formed by the French river system. These natural lines have been strengthened with both field and permanent installations, and particularly with obstacles of all types. Key terrain throughout the area no doubt has been strengthened in every possible way. Individual fortifications, which are not laid out as densely as in the West Wall and follow no apparent zone system, have been reported in great numbers, particularly in the neighborhood of communication centers. Available information on the distinguishable lines is indicated on the map, figure 1 (facing p. 142).

b. The Maginot Line

By the terms of the armistice between Germany and France the Maginot Line became a part of the German western defenses. All reports agree that some portions of the Maginot Line have been abandoned while others which are strategically and tactically useful to the Germans are being steadily reinforced and incorporated into the West Wall system.

Reports that the Maginot Line has been altered to face westward are patently false, since most of the French works were sited on forward slopes facing eastward. It can be assumed, however, that every effort has been put forth by the Germans to incorporate useful French fortifications into their West Wall system, and that those works which cannot be used offensively will serve as an additional, highly developed band of concrete and steel obstacles in front of the West Wall itself.

15. EASTERN LAND DEFENSES

a. Eastern System

The German "Eastern System" of fortifications, which faces the Polish provinces of Posen and Pomerania, is a deep zone of modern, permanent works. It was built primarily as a strategic base for operations in Poland, and secondarily as security for Germany's rear during operations in France and the Lowlands. The keystone of the "Eastern System" is a quadrilateral area due east of Berlin on the Polish frontier, measuring about 40 miles long from north to south and 20 miles from west to east. Because of its shape and the river on which it is based, it is also known as the "Oder Quadrilateral." This system, by providing security for the German center during the Polish campaign, effectively prevented any Polish movement against Berlin, and permitted the Germans to mass the bulk of their armies on the Polish flanks in German Pomerania, in Prussia in the north, and in Silesia in the south. Without this system as a pivot, the German Army could not have executed its bold double envelopment of the Polish armies without the greatest risk.

The Oder Quadrilateral is reported to be supplemented by minor belts of permanent works in Pomerania, north of the Netze River, and in the vicinity of Schneidemühl, and in Silesia, northeast of Glogau and Breslau. There is no available information as to their extent.

b. Slovakian Treaty Line

By virtue of a "treaty" concluded between Germany and Slovakia in March 1939, Germany was given the right to fortify the White Carpathian mountain range to a depth of 30 miles within Slovakian territory. It is not known whether this system has actually been built.

c. The East Wall

A report dated February 1943, states that a new "Ostwall" system of fortifications, planned and recommended by the German High Command, had been approved for construction. There is no definite evidence that construction has been started, nor of the nature of the proposed fortifications; however, the general areas that were covered by the treaty are shown on the map, figure 1 (facing p. 142).

d. East Prussian System

The East Prussian fortifications appear to have been started secretly during the Versailles Treaty era, and were greatly strengthened during 1938 and 1939 by the addition of many forts, individual bunkers, blockhouses, tank obstacles, and wire entanglements. The strategic purpose of the system was similar to that of the "Eastern System"; in addition, it was expected to protect industries in East Prussia.

The East Prussian works may be divided into two groups: one facing south against Poland, the other running in a north-south direction along the general line of the Angerapp River. The fortified area of Lötzen forms the junction of these two lines. In the southern system, a very large number of "bunkers" were observed under construction late in 1938, and therefore the strength of this part of the line is believed to be great. This southern system extends along the general line of Osterode—Tannenberg—Ortelsburg—Spirding See—Lötzen.

Section V. THE WEST WALL

16. SCOPE OF THE SYSTEM

a. General

The West Wall, the principal system of German fortifications, faces a part of the Netherlands, Belgium, Luxembourg, France, and a part of Switzerland. It was intended to serve as the base for offensive operations against the western powers and to provide strategic defense during operations in the east. Secondarily, the system had the defensive role of protecting vital industrial areas, such as the iron and coal mines of the Saar; the lead and zinc mills in the southern Schwarzwald; and the industrial areas of Ludwigshafen, Mannheim, and the Rhineland.

Late in 1942 the German Defense Ministry established a Western Defense Command to take over control of both the West Wall and the Maginot Line.

One-third of all the construction facilities of Germany and more than 500,000 men were concentrated on the task of constructing the West Wall. The great majority of these men were civilian workers, but troops were used on roads, camouflage, signal communications, and field fortifications. The project was carried out by the *Organisation Todt,* a semimilitary construction corps, which began the work in 1938. The Todt organization controlled 15,000 trucks during the construction operations. At the outbreak of war in September 1939, 6,000,000 tons of concrete,

48

260,000,000 board feet of lumber, and 3,000,000 rolls of barbed wire were among the materials already used in the fortifications.

The depth of the fortified areas of the West Wall ranges from 8 to 20 miles. The length of the line is about 350 miles. Within these limits the whole great project in 1939 encompassed 22,000 separate fortified works—which means an average density of about 1 fort on each 28 yards of front. The average distance between works, in depth, is 200 to 600 yards. The actual spacing of the works depends, of course, on the nature of the terrain, and U. S. observers who have visited some parts of the fortifications have reported that the space between them varied from 200 to 1,000 yards.

These figures are merely statistical and are useful only in giving an idea of the vastness of the project. A full appreciation of the military value of the West Wall can be gained only by considering the tactical and strategic layout of its zones and component fortifications in relation to the terrain and the mission for which they were designed.

b. Distinguishable Lines

The West Wall consists of a series of deep fortified zones rather than a line of forts and includes individual steel and concrete works, field entrenchments, belts of wire, and tank obstacles. An example of the actual outline of these zones, showing how they are adapted to the terrain, is shown in figure 2 (facing p. 142), which is a map of a sector of the West

Wall. The following individual fortified lines may be distinguished in the West Wall system:

(1) The "Rhine Line" runs from a point south of Karlsruhe to Basle.

(2) The "Black Forest Line" is a reserve position for the "Rhine Line" along the crest of the Black Forest (Schwarzwald).

(3) The "Saar-Pfalz Line" extends from a point on the Moselle River southwest of Trier through Saarburg—Merzig—Dudweiler—St. Ingbert—a point south of Zweibrücken—a point south of Pirmasens—Bergzabern—Bienwald.

(4) The "Saarbrücken Line" is an advanced line in front of the "Saar-Pfalz Line" extending through Merzig—Saarbrücken—St. Ingbert.

(5) The "Hunsrück Line" is a reserve position for the "Saar-Pfalz Line," extending from a point just east of Trier through St. Wendel—a point south of Landstuhl—Landau—a point on the Rhine south of Germersheim.

(6) The "Eifel Line" runs from the junction of the Moselle River and the Luxembourg frontier at Wasserbillig, along the Luxembourg frontier to its junction with Belgium—thence along the crest of the Schneifel hills to Schleiden.

(7) The "Aachen Positions" consist of two lines. An advanced line runs from Monschau through Rötgen—a point due east of Aachen—Herzogenrath, north of Aachen, at which point it joins the main line. The main line extends from Schleiden through Steckenborn—Stolberg—Herzogenrath.

(8) The "Holland Position" extends from Herzogenrath through Geilenkirchen—a point east of Erkelenz—a point 12 miles due west of Munich-Gladbach.

17. ZONE ORGANIZATION

The West Wall is divided into zones of defensive belts in depth, especially in terrain which favors an enemy attack. This is a part of the German doctrine of defense.

A sector of the West Wall will normally consist, in the order named, of the following four areas (see fig. 3):

a. Advance Position (Field Fortifications)

The advance position is an area of field fortifications, including trenches, barbed-wire entanglements, machine-gun emplacements, observation posts, and artillery emplacements.

b. Fortified Belt

This belt is from 2,000 to 4,000 yards deep, and consists of concrete and steel works and artillery emplacements the weapons of which completely cover the zone area with mutually supporting fire. The forward boundary of this belt is 5,000 to 10,000 yards in the rear of the advanced position.

c. Second Fortified Belt

This belt is similar to the first, but in general it is not so strong. It is located 10,000 to 15,000 yards in the rear of the first fortified belt. In the intermediate terrain between the two fortified belts, fortified works

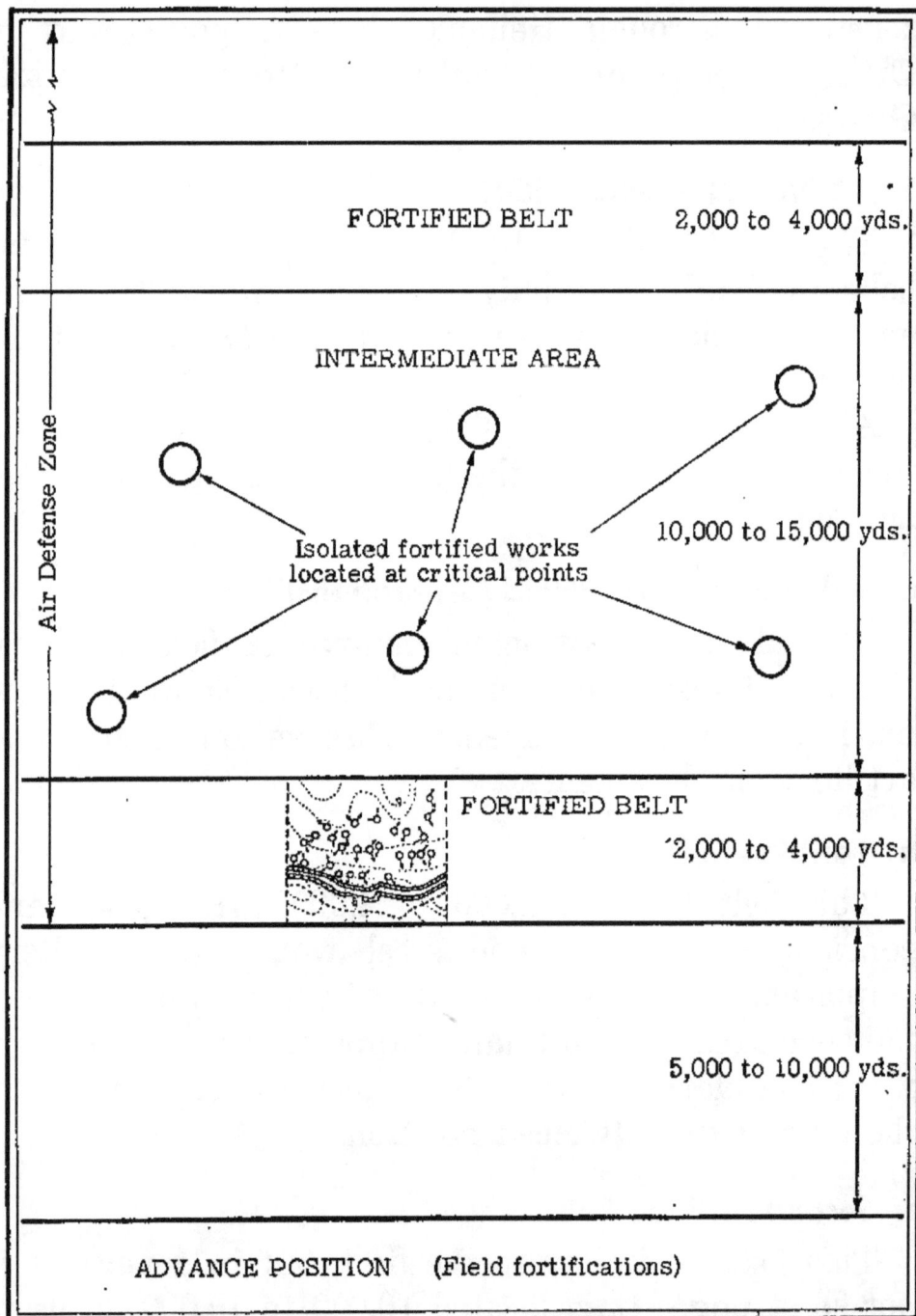

Figure 3.—Organization of a fortified zone.

are located at critical points on natural avenues of advance.

d. Air Defense Zone

The air defense zone comprises the first and second fortified belts and an area extending from 10 to 30 miles in rear of the second belt. This constitutes the so-called "ring of steel" around Germany. This zone has antiaircraft defenses throughout, but the greater part of the antiaircraft matériel is in the area behind the second fortified belt. An efficient warning system is maintained, and attack planes and balloon barrages complement the antiaircraft artillery.

The massing of the major part of the antiaircraft defenses in the rear of the second fortified belt, the Germans believe, produces optimum results by making possible the concentration of the bulk of antiaircraft fire on hostile aircraft.

It is not believed, however, that all areas of the West Wall are divided invariably into a fixed number of belts. The defenses are adapted to local topography. Where the terrain is defensively strong, as for instance in the Vosges Mountains, only a minimum development of artificial works will probably be found. But it must be emphasized that in the natural avenues of invasion into Germany the zone organization of fortifications will be encountered in great strength.

18. DETAILS OF A ZONE

Accurate and detailed representations of the known fortifications in the areas indicated by rectangles on the large fortifications map (fig. 2, facing p. 142) are

marked on five large-scale maps of parts of the West
Wall (figs. 4, 6, 7, 8, 9). The nature and location of
the defenses on the terrain are shown, but the direction
of fire of the active works are unknown. A study of
the maps will reveal excellent adaptation of the works
to the terrain, great density of fortified works on weak
ground, continuous lines of obstacles, and adequate
and strongly defended communications.

Actual aerial photographs of a part of the Otterbach
sector of the West Wall are shown in figure 5 ① and ②,
and they match the terrain in the lower middle part of
figure 4. An interpretive sketch of this area has been
made in figure 5 ③.

The sector includes:

a. A continuous band of antitank obstacles.

b. Continuous bands of wire entanglements.

c. A deep area of fortified works, the fire from
which covers the obstacles and all the terrain.

d. Fortified shelters, without armament, for quar-
tering troops.

e. Artillery emplacements.

The density of the fortified works in this sector is
28 forts in 700 yards of front, or 1 for every 25 yards.
The average distance between works is 75 yards. It is
not believed, however, that this is a typical section of
the West Wall, but rather that this terrain, favoring
attack, required defensive works very closely spaced.
The depth of the installation is less than the 2,000- to
4,000-yard depth mentioned in paragraph **17b**, above,
and it is probable that only part of the zone is shown.
On the other hand, the defense of the terrain at this
point may have been made most effective by the close

spacing of the forts rather than by disposing them in greater depth. The Germans are not bound by copybook rules but always adapt their defenses to the terrain.

As one stands in front of the defenses, the fact that there are numerous forts is not visually apparent. (See fig. 10, p. 62, below. The defenses are normally not so visible as those pictured in this illustration.) The

Figure 4.—Plotted area No. 1 (Otterbach sector).

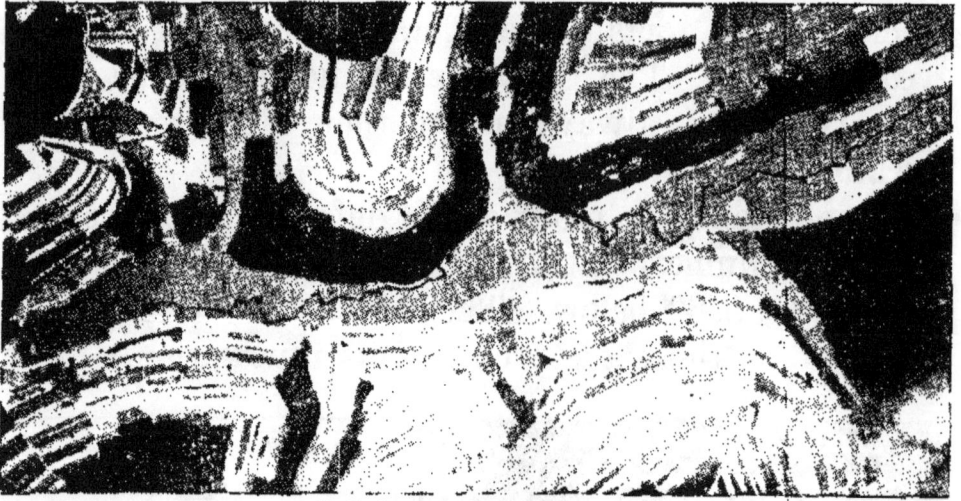

① Before work was started.

② Work in progress.

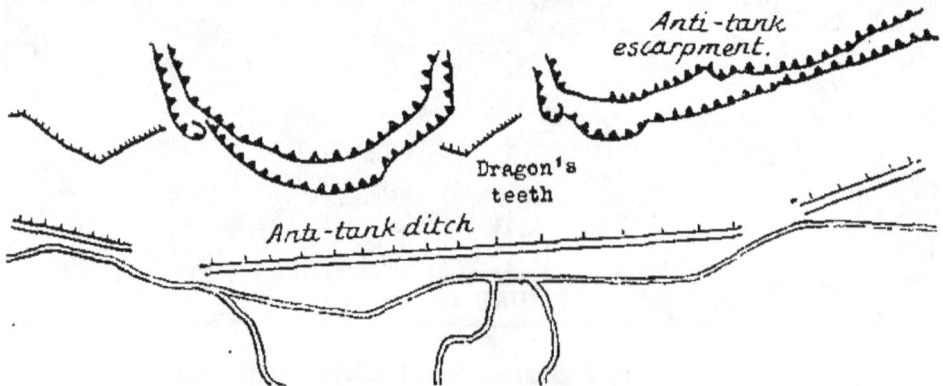

④ Interpretation of photograph.

Figure 5.—Aerial photographs plotted in figure 4.

FORTIFICATIONS

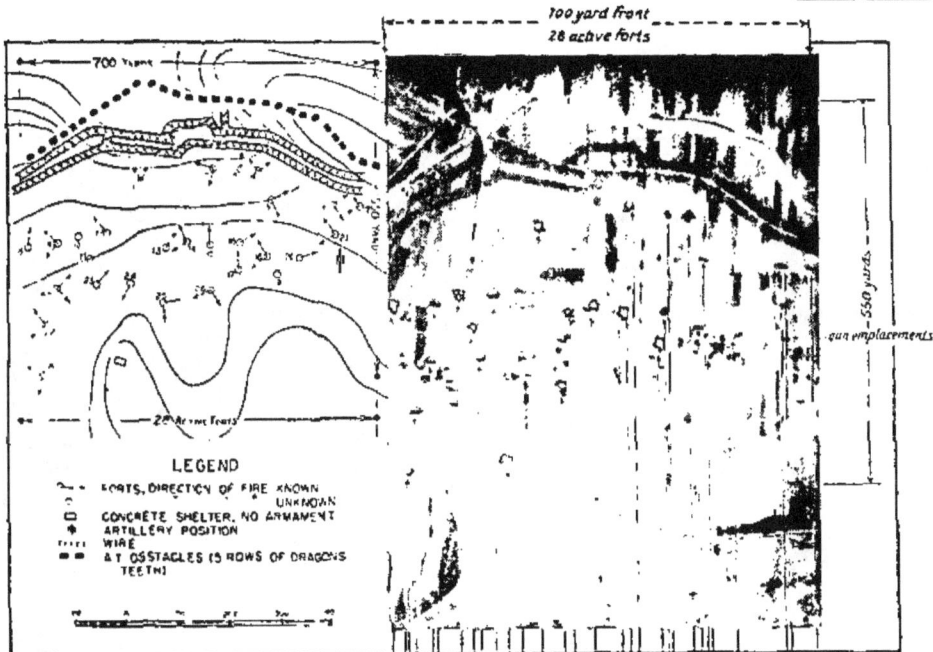

Other patterns observed.

(a) Small machine gun forts

(b) Forts with two embrasures.

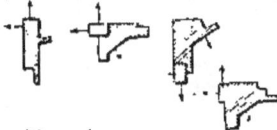

(c) Forts with cupolas.

(d) Gun emplacements

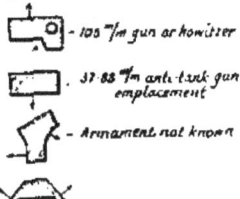

- 105 ⁷/ₘ gun or howitzer

- 37·83 ⁷/ₘ anti-tank gun emplacement

- Armament not known

(e) Shelters without armament

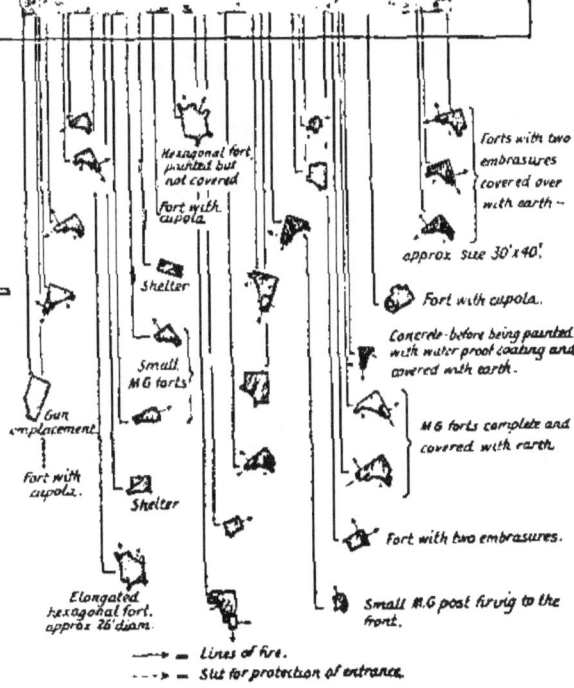

① Aerial photograph of another part of the Otterbach sector.

Figure 5 (continued).—Aerial photographs plotted in figure 4.

Figure 6.—Plotted area No. 2.

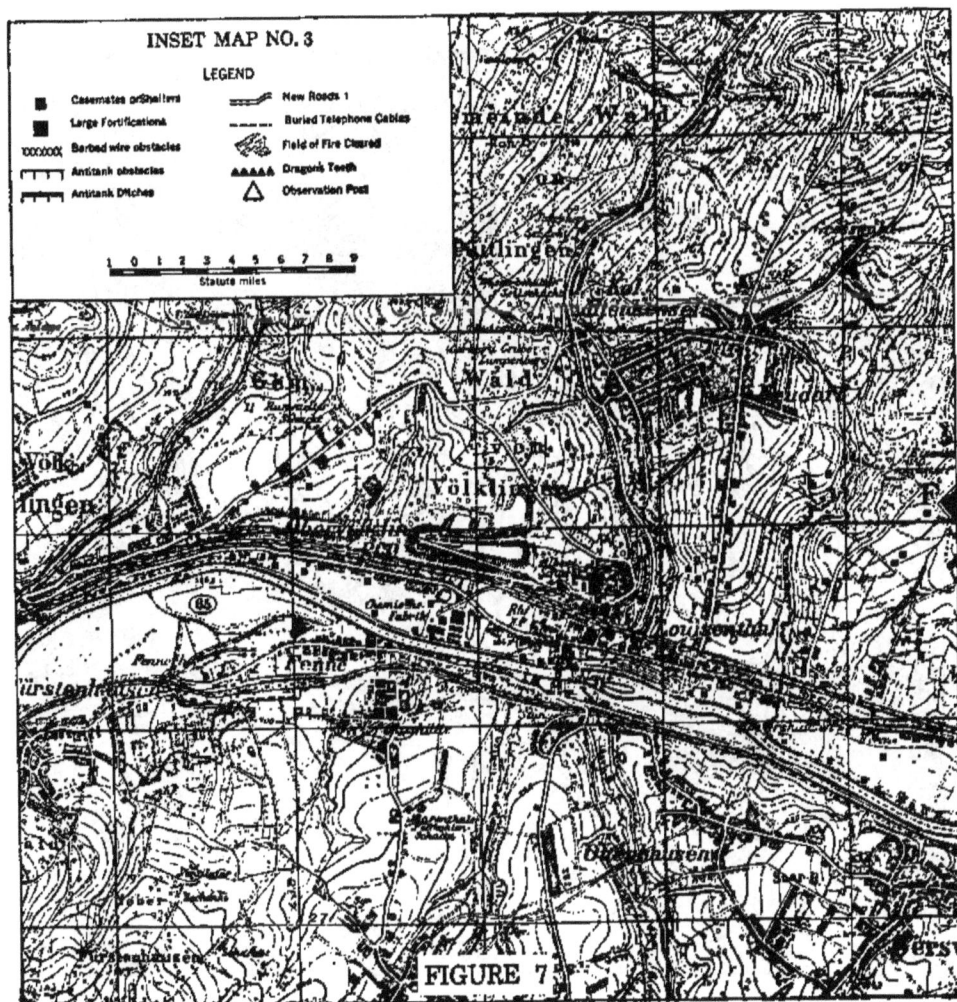

Figure 7.—Plotted area No. 3.

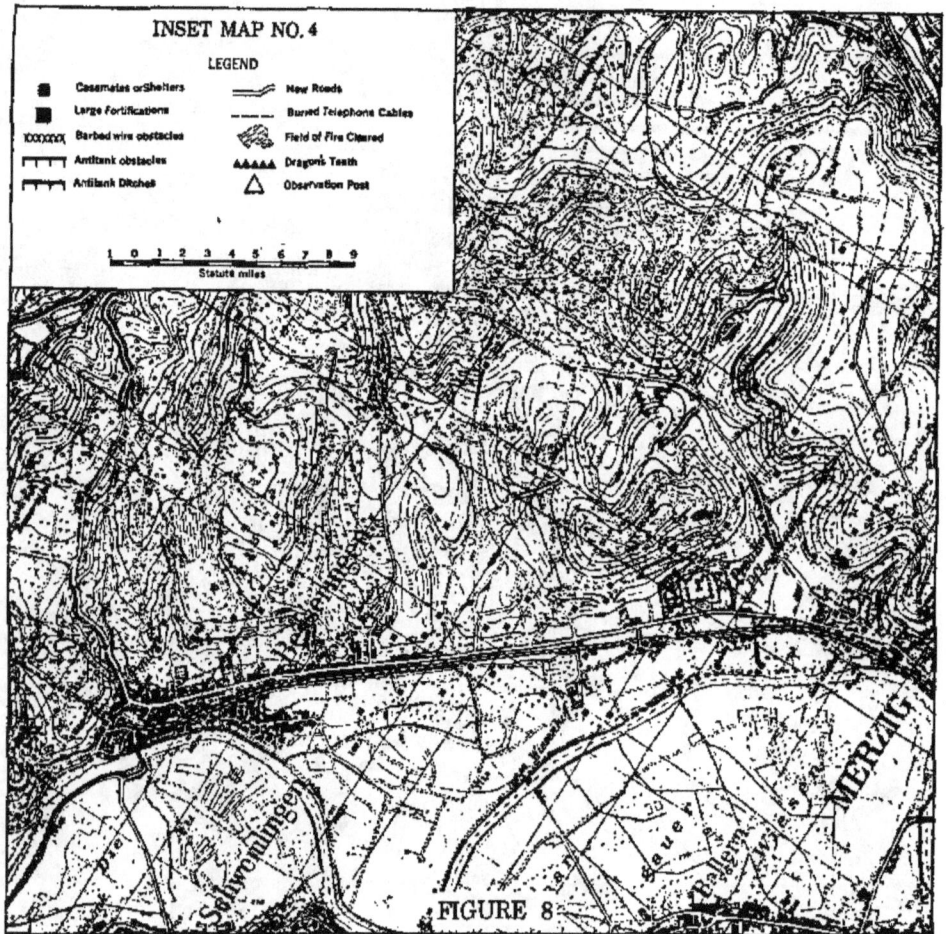

Figure 8.—Plotted area No. 4.

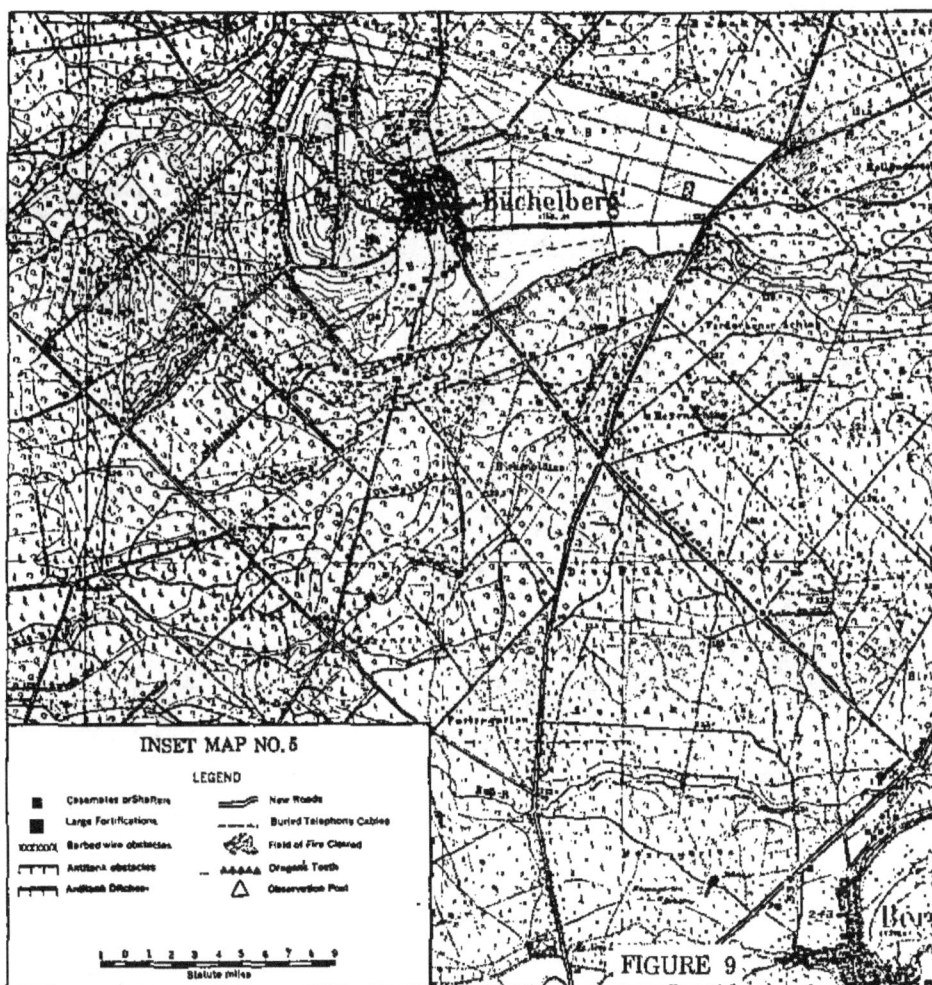

INSET MAP NO. 5

LEGEND

Figure 9.—Plotted area No. 5.

concrete works have been earth-covered; the ground has been graded to provide grazing fire; and the completed installation has been so integrated into the topography as almost to escape notice. Thus an attacking force may not be able to spot defending

Figure 10.—Works concealed in terrain.

centers of resistance readily, a fact which may encourage doubts and hesitation as to where to concentrate heavy, indirect artillery fire. Furthermore, bunkers are so widely separated that fire which misses one will not hit another.

19. PERMANENT FORTIFICATIONS

a. Types of Works

The West Wall in general contains two kinds of fortified works: the decentralized type and the closed type. The decentralized type consists of a group of mutually supporting concrete bunkers or steel turrets united into a center of resistance that is capable of continuous machine-gun and antitank fire. In other words, a work of the decentralized type is characterized by firepower. The separate bunkers are often interconnected by tunnels to facilitate the relief of personnel, the supply of ammunition, and the care and removal of the wounded.

The term "closed type" is applied to strong underground shelters of concrete which have no emplacements for guns. These works have the important function of sheltering large bodies of infantry and reserves from air and artillery bombardment. At the proper time the waiting reserves are committed fresh from the shelters in a counterattack to drive back the enemy and to restore the position. The closed type of fortification is also used for relieving units and for the storage of ammunition. Lacking firepower, the shelters are protected by obstacles and field works. Whatever the differences in characteristics, both the decentralized type and the closed type have one important feature in common: they are intended to hold ground against the enemy's maximum effort. In the accomplishment of this mission, these permanent works are complemented by extensive field fortifications which add flexibility to the defense. The field works are occupied during engagements by the troops who are sheltered in the closed type of fortifications. (German field fortifications are discussed in par. **24**, p. 95, below.)

b. Thickness of Concrete and Armor

The protective thickness of concrete walls and roofs of the works in the West Wall is reported to range from 5 to 10 feet. During inspection trips, U. S. military attachés were told that the minimum thickness of the concrete was 5 feet, and it is believed that important works at critical locations may have thicknesses up to 10 feet. However, there are less massive works, some photographs indicating that certain walls are as thin as 3 feet. The armor of steel turrets is estimated to be from 7 to 10 inches thick. These figures are only approximate. Comparative figures compiled by a reliable source in 1939 indicate a lower average thickness. According to this source, the average thickness of concrete and loophole armor was increased in new works in 1939 as follows:

	1938	*1939*
Walls and roofs_____	5 feet	6 feet 8 inches
Armor plate in loopholes_____	3⅞ inches	7⅞ inches

Some of the materials used in new works built in 1939 are given in the list below. A quick-setting cement was used. There is no reliable data as to what water-cement ratio was employed, but it was reported to be a sloppy mix. Forms were removed 5 to 6 days after the cement was poured. The concrete for foundation, walls, and anti-mining aprons, when the latter were used, was poured monolithically. According to one report, the minimum crushing resistance of the concrete was 3,550 pounds per square inch. Steel rods for reinforcing the concrete were distributed uniformly by weaving them in metal mats that were laid in the concrete as indicated in **c** (2) below.

c. Table of Materials

Cubic feet

(1) Approximate constituents (one cubic meter (35.3 cubic feet) of mixed concrete:

Gravel or broken stone, ⅜ to 1⅝ inches	24
Fine gravel, ¼ to ½ inch	14
Sand, up to ⅛ inch	7
Cement	12⅓
	[1] 57⅓

(2) Horizontal and vertical steel mats with reinforcing rods:

Diameter of bars ---- ½ to ⅝ inch.
Spacing of bars in mats ---- 6 inches.
Horiontal or vertical intervals between mats ---- 10 inches.

(3) Steel joists used as additional reinforcement in roofs:

Size ---- 8 to 10 inches in depth.
Spacing ---- 12 to 18 inches.
Ceilings ---- The lower flanges of the steel joists support steel plates, ⁷⁄₃₂ of an inch thick, to form permanently fixed sheathing in the ceiling.

---

[1] The actual cubic-foot contents exceeds the volume of the constituents in a cubic meter. This is due to the fact that materials of finer texture, such as sand and cement, fill in the interstices of the gravel

(4) Doors_____ Outer doors were made of 1½-inch steel plates, 4 feet high and 2 feet 7 inches wide. In exceptional cases doors were made of timber, 1⅛ inches thick, faced on both sides with one-eighth-inch steel plates. The latter doors measure 6 feet 3 inches by 2 feet 7 inches. Some large emplacements were reported to have steel doors, folding in two leaves, which were 4 feet 7 inches, or 5 feet 3 inches, high, by 6 feet 7 inches wide.

(5) Lighting_____ Along the Rhine, the emplacements are lighted by acetylene or paraffin. In some cases electric lighting has been reported.

(6) Telephones_____ Large-scale installations of telephones have been reported. The terminals are fixed in an opening outside the fortification, near the entrance.

d. Strengthening of Old Works

Some of the original works of the West Wall were reinforced in 1939, chiefly by the addition around their bases of concrete aprons faced with steel sheet piling (fig. 11) and by superimposing new, reinforced concrete walls over the original front walls. The aprons have been installed principally around emplacements on the banks of the Rhine, and for this reason it is believed that they are intended to protect the foundation against flood erosion as well as against the mining action of near-misses of heavy artillery and bombs. Probably the reinforcing project was undertaken not only because the Germans reached the conclusion that

Figure 11.—Steel sheet piling added to casemate. (Note also the coping at the corners, and the camouflage anchor hooks.)

the concrete was not sufficiently thick, but also because of the hurried nature of the original construction.

The thickness of the aprons, which were cast in steel sheet piling, was estimated at 3 feet 4 inches, while that of the added walls ranged between 3 feet 4 inches to 5 feet. The added walls were not reinforced with steel.

20. DECENTRALIZED FORTIFICATIONS
a. Description

A U. S. officer examined one of the so-called decentralized fortifications on the west bank of the Obra River. It was located on a 30-foot ridge which ran within 200 yards of the river and parallel to it (fig. 12). Three well-camouflaged six-port turrets were spaced about 200 yards apart on high points on the ridge. The field of fire immediately around the ridge had been cleared of forest growth. Each turret was surrounded by barbed-wire entanglements, usually extending 50 or more yards away. The entanglements had gates for facilitating movement to and from the turret entrances.

At a lower level, covering a bridge across the Obra, was a concrete bunker which was also part of this system. Our attaché was told that the number of turrets and pillboxes of any such fortification depends upon the terrain and the mission, but that it was usual for each fortification to have three six-port turrets; the central turret was used for command and the flanking turrets for artillery and infantry observers, in addition to normal fire missions. Usually each turret has two antitank guns and four machine guns. Each bunker has an antitank and one or more machine guns. Each fortification has all-around protection. The entire fortification is manned by 50 to 100 men.

Each of the three main turrets is the station of an observer, one for command, one for infantry, and one for artillery. The Germans place great stress on the value of information. The observers are stationed in

Six port turret
(Command Post)

Bridge

Six port turret
(Artillery observer)

Enemy

Six port turret
(Infantry observer)

Bunker

Entrance

Entrance

Entrance

PLAN

①

Turret

Entrance

Bunker

SIDE ELEVATION

②

Entrance to turret
and tunnels to bunkers

Turret

Turret

Ridge Line

(Estimated 10 to 13 ft below surface)

1st Level

2nd Level

Personnel, kitchen,
and toilets.

Power plant and two
independent tunnels
connecting turrets.

3rd Level

4th Level

Ammunition

ELEVATION

③

Not drawn to scale.

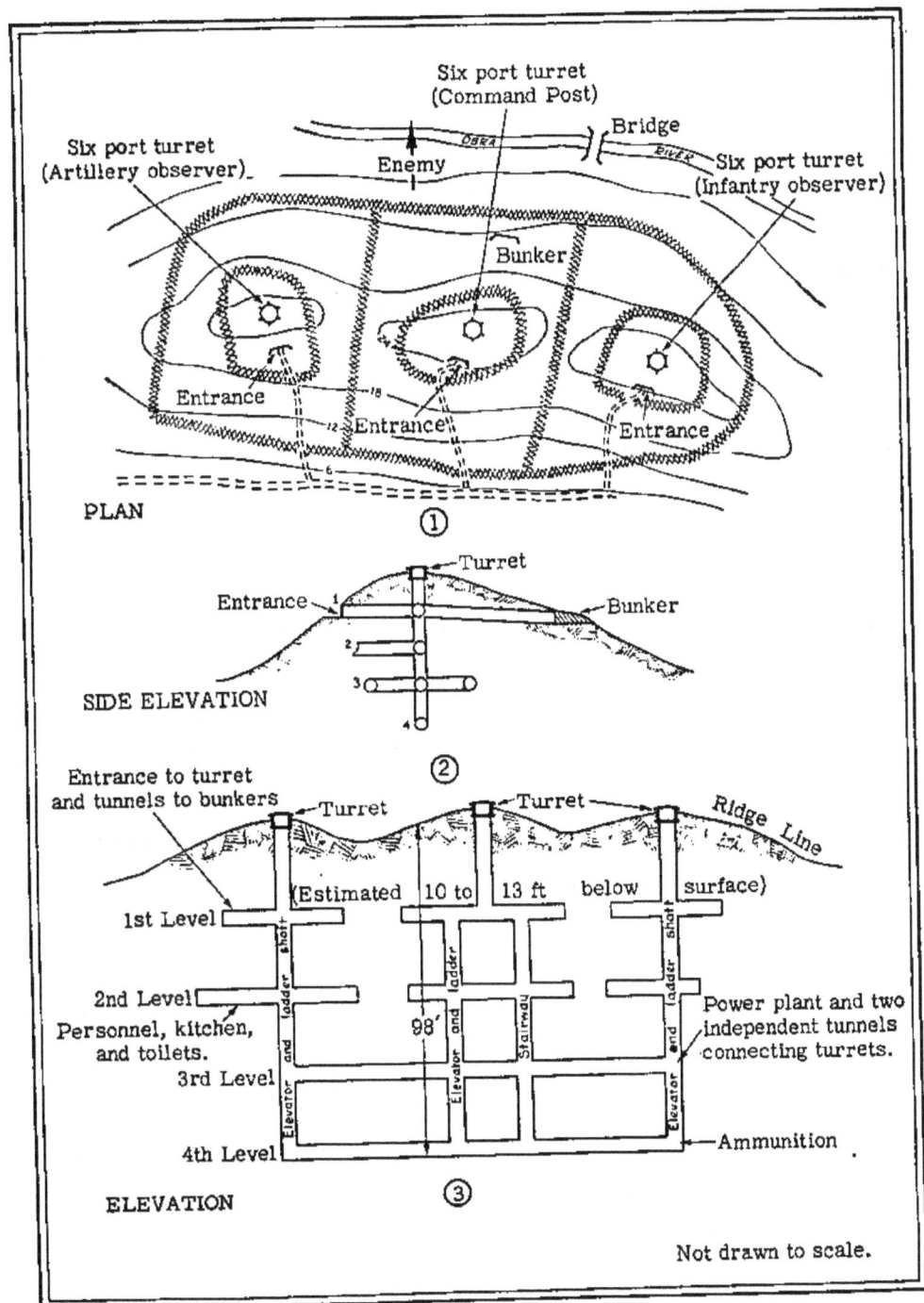

Figure 12.—Decentralized fortification.

these forward turrets to keep the sector commander and important subordinates in constant touch with the situation.

Two similar fortifications were sited on a parallel ridge about 600 yards to the rear, covering the flanks of the fortifications shown. Apparently these fortifications were placed to cover the ground between fortifications on the first line. It is not known how deep or extensive the system was in this locality. Considerable timber was in the area, and it is believed that the entire ground area was not covered by fire. Dead areas were covered by the usual temporary field fortifications. The fortifications apparently did not interfere with the normal road net. Friendly artillery and infantry troops could move easily through the fortified area.

The entrance to a typical six-port turret was of concrete. It was on a reverse slope and well camouflaged. The horizontal distance between the entrance and the turret varied from 10 to 25 yards in the works that were seen.

The entrance was an oval opening in a concrete face (protected by a concrete overhang) about 5 feet high and 3 feet wide, covered by an armored door 2 inches thick. The door was protected by flanking machine-gun fire from openings in the wings of the entrance face. These wings were really two separate pillboxes which formed part of the entrance. The Germans state that these doors are gasproof (they have rubber lips or gaskets), and are capable of withstanding fairly heavy detonations.

An interesting feature of this entrance was that strong wire nets projected 15 inches from the face of the concrete walls of the entrance and above the openings. The purpose of these wire nets is not exactly clear. One German officer said that it was to catch debris which might clog up the entrances; another said that it was to prevent an enemy who had gained access to the top of the fortification from effectively employing hand grenades or gasoline bombs, or firing into the openings. However, the fact that the netting would be destroyed by a hand grenade does not fully support the second explanation.

The firing port covering the entrance was in the general form of a truncated pyramid with its walls constructed in five steps, each narrower than the next. By this means the opening presents approximately perpendicular faces to any direct fire entering the port. The Germans claim that this prevents both spatter and ricochet of bullets or fragments into the opening.

The main air-intake ports are located on the face of the concrete entrance wall. They are two in number, circular in shape, about 8 inches in diameter, and are protected by strong metal gratings. In addition to these, each turret or bunker has its own air-intake valves for emergency use. These are a possible weakness if they are attacked by hand-placed explosives and grenades.

On entering the fortification one crosses a pit trap door about 12 feet deep, designed to trap an enemy who has forced the entrance. The trap door is controlled from inside the fort. Immediately inside the

entrance is a degassing room which consists principally of a shower bath. All doors throughout the
fortification are airtight, and in some instances, especially near the entrance, double doors are installed.
Booby traps will be encountered when these fortifications are attacked; they will probably be installed in
advance and will require only simple arming as the
defenders leave through tunnels. Occasionally, underground pillboxes are employed to cover tunnels with
machine-gun fire.

The fortification is built around two vertical shafts
somewhat offset from the center turret. One of
these shafts contains a double elevator; the second
shaft consists of a spiral staircase and two steel lad-
ders for emergency. Horizontal tunnels extend from
these shafts in four levels, of which the deepest is 90
feet underground. The topmost level comprises tunnels leading to the entrance and to bunkers; the
second level from the top is for personnel, kitchen,
and toilets; the third level contains the power plant,
the main gas filters, water pumps, and two independent tunnels to each of the two six-port flanking turrets. The U. S. attaché was not taken to the lowest
level but was told that this contained ammunition
storerooms and water pumps.

Each turret, each bunker, and each of the rooms in
which personnel must function in action contain individual dust and gas filters which are normally operated by electric motors, but which are also provided
with a hand crank for emergency operation in case a
part of the fortification is isolated from the main

source of electric power. Special attention has been given to the problems that would arise if the bunker were isolated by enemy action.

There are more concrete bunkers in the West Wall than steel turrets, and there is a considerable variation between the types of concrete bunkers. Some are round and others are square and boxlike. All concrete bunkers and steel turrets, however, are coated with a very effective camouflage surface which blends their angular shapes into the terrain.

b. Steel Turrets

All the turrets seen by U. S. officers were of the six-port type and were estimated to be from 7 to 10 inches thick (figs. 13, 14, and 15). The turrets do not revolve; the Germans, unlike the French, do not consider revolving or disappearing turrets to be practical because they are complicated mechanisms that are put out of action rather easily by gunfire. Figure 13 illustrates a type of observation turret known to exist in the West Wall. Steel inserts fit into the ports and provide additional protection for instruments and small arms. These inserts may be removed by hand in a few seconds.

Turrets may be used independently, particularly on ridge lines, but they are more often mounted in the roofs of concrete pillboxes to provide all-around observation and supporting small arms fire. The ceiling of the steel turret is often painted in colored sections corresponding to various fields of fire for the defending weapons. Previously prepared plans of

fire are thus simplified and insured against error in
the stress of battle.   The armament of a six-port turret is normally 2 antitank guns and 4 machine guns,
and the crew consists of 6 to 10 men.

Figure 13.—Six-port steel turret.

Observation in a steel turret is possible, even when all
firing ports are closed and gasproofed by sliding steel
blocks, by means of a periscope such as is illustrated
in figures 14 and 15.

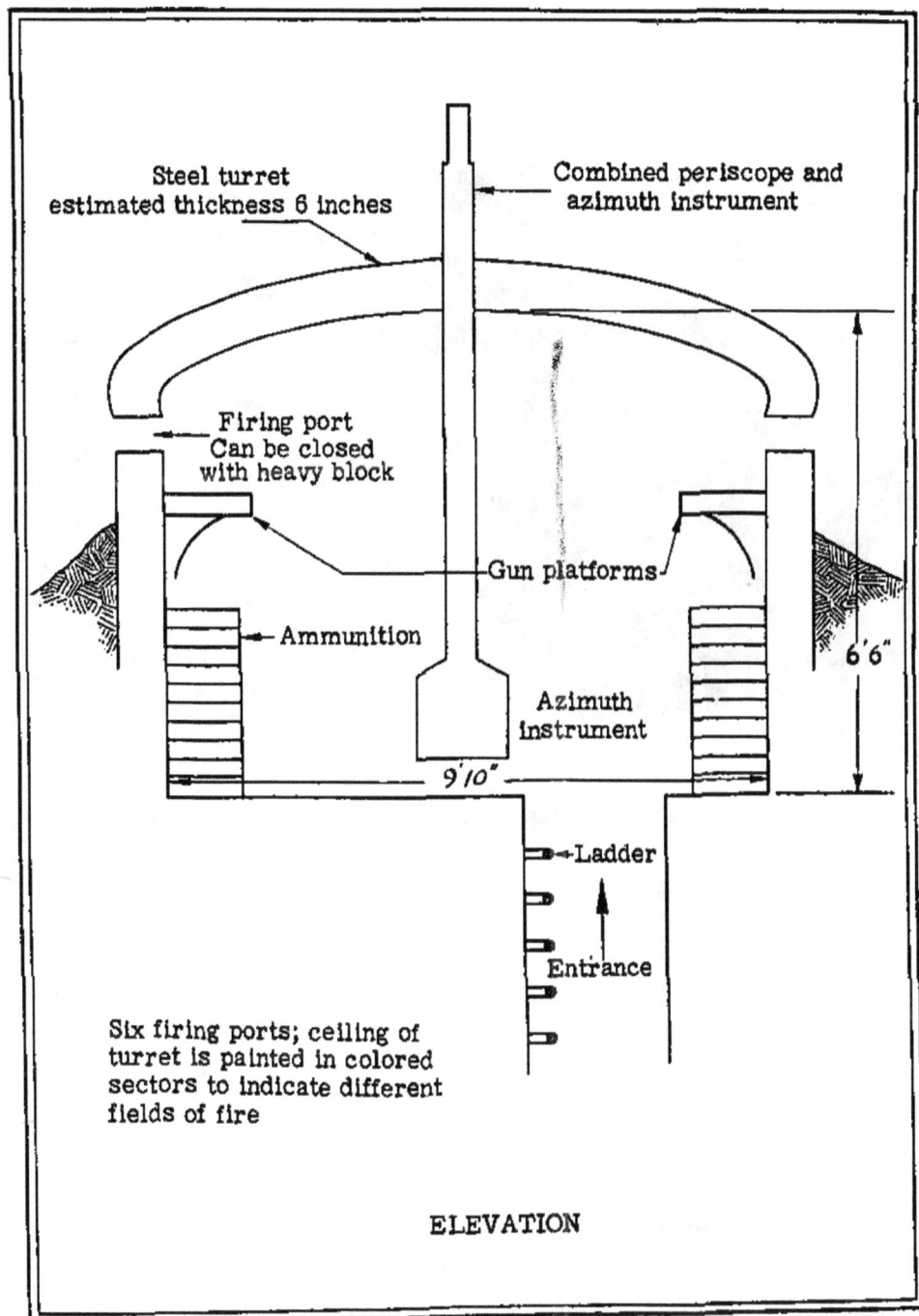

Steel turret
estimated thickness 6 inches

Combined periscope and
azimuth instrument

Firing port
Can be closed
with heavy block

Gun platforms

Ammunition

Azimuth
instrument

9'10"

6'6"

Ladder

Entrance

Six firing ports; ceiling of
turret is painted in colored
sectors to indicate different
fields of fire

ELEVATION

Figure 14.—Observation turret.

Figure 15.—Camouflaged six-port turret, with periscope.

c. Concrete Pillboxes

The interior plan of a small concrete pillbox is shown in figure 16. The majority of the fortified works in the German defenses are of concrete. It may also be expected that in the zones of fortifications nearer the coast of France concrete works will predominate, because steel is a critical material for Germany. Undoubtedly, most of the German steel will go into weapons and projectiles and comparatively very little into fortifications.

The walls of pyramidal embrasure openings are stepped (see fig. 17) so as to cut down the probability of ricochet of enemy projectiles through the port.

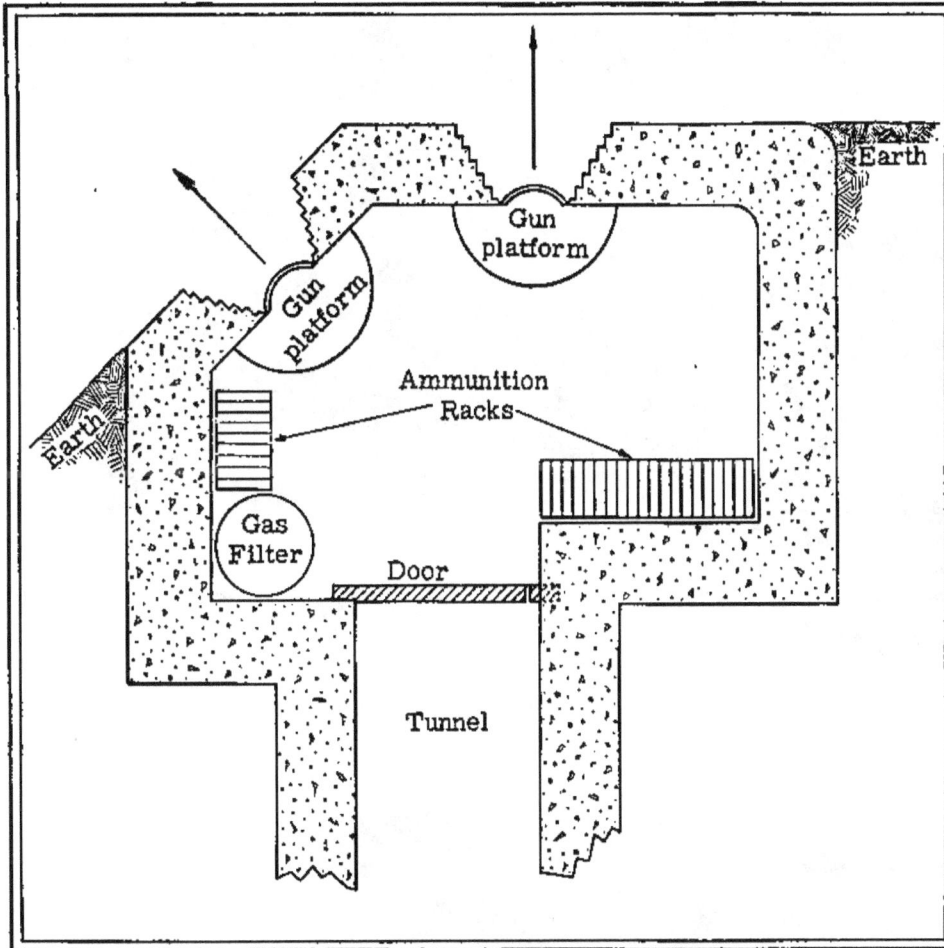

Figure 16.—Plan of concrete pillbox.

Most of the firing ports are made for the use of gun-shields as shown in figure 18, but the less important works do not include such refinements. The light-gauge metal cover shown in the lowered position in figure 17 is evidently intended as protection against observation and the weather rather than against hostile fire. Embrasures of more recent construction, particularly in thin walls, often feature plane faces of heavy armor plate, which require small ports and consequently offer small targets to hostile direct fire.

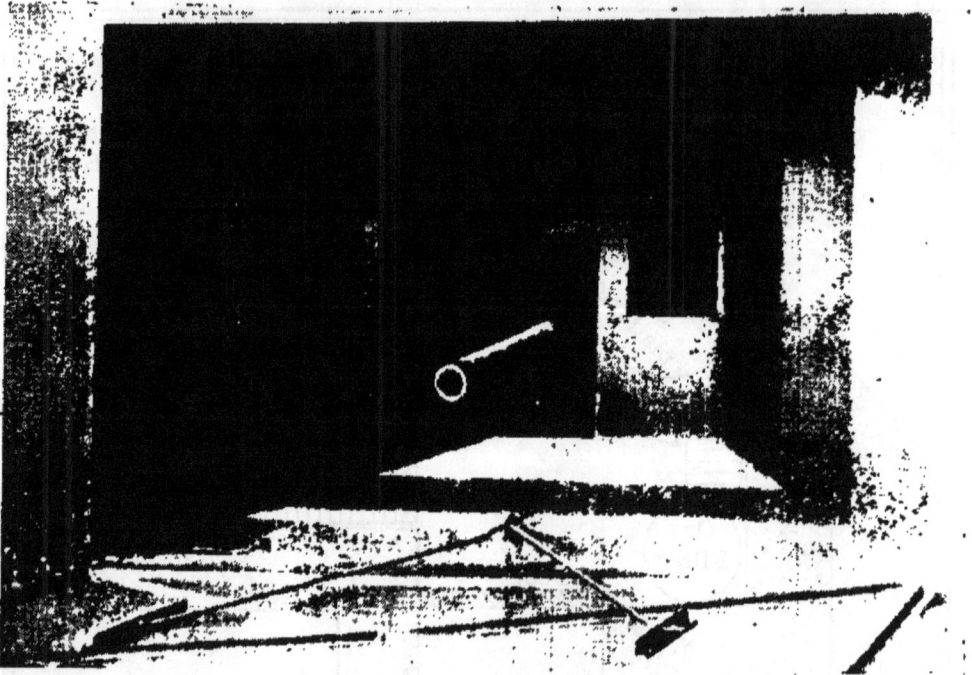

Figure 17.—Stepped embrasure opening.

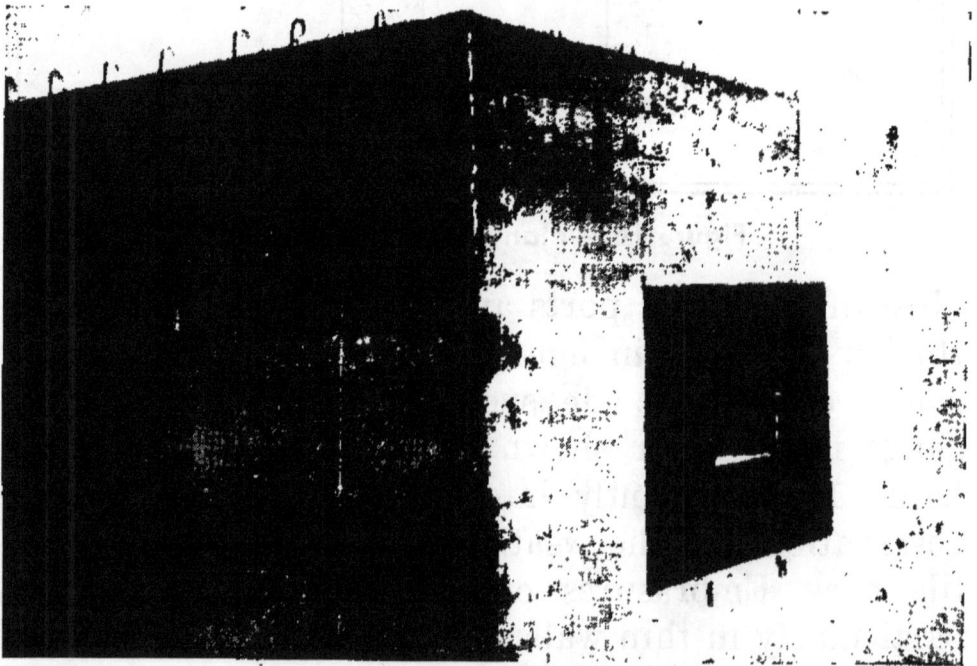

Figure 18.—Firing port with gun shield.

Figure 19, illustrating this type of embrasure, indicates also the difficulty of blending the appearance of the steel plate into the concrete background. The work shown in figure 19 utilizes both the plane and the stepped embrasure design. It is probable that this design was not original with the structure, but was forced by the addition of the anti-mining apron to

Figure 19.—Armored embrasure with stepped apron.

the old work. Figure 20 is a photograph of the interior of a machine-gun embrasure which has no apparent provision for a protective shield.

d. Weapons and Fortress Troops

Weapons are habitually kept inside the turrets and bunkers, but the majority of these weapons are removable to field fortifications (see fig. 21), and are the normal equipment of organizations of the field army which bring in the weapons when they are ordered to garrison the defenses. The pintles or trunnions are built into the fortifications. A few of the weapons for which emplacement is essential to the defense are permanently mounted in the forts. To care for these weapons and to act as skeleton garrisons and

Figure 20.—Machine-gun embrasure (interior view).

caretaking detachments, a small proportion of troops are kept permanently assigned to fortified zones. These troops are very important to the defense because of their intimate knowledge of the forts, their familiarity with the surrounding terrain, and their

Figure 21.——Machine-gun crew leaving bunker. (Note the standard machine gun being removed.)

training in prepared plans for defensive action and counterattack. They act as key personnel to insure optimum use of the fortifications by units from the field army, which form the main part of the garrison in case of defensive combat.

The ports in many instances have sliding steel blocks to permit closure and gasproofing. In some instances, particularly in the larger pillboxes, there will be walls within the pillboxes separating the interior into compartments. These are intended to cut down casualties if direct hits are made in an embrasure opening, or if a wall is perforated by gunfire.

The pillboxes are normally sited on forward slopes and recessed into the sides of hills in terrain compartments and corridors. This arrangement permits effective camouflage by means of earth cover. Some of these works will be sited on reverse slopes. The Germans plan their installations for all-around fire; their defenses are almost as strong on the flanks and rear as on the front. Very rarely will concrete forts be found on ridges; where the terrain is flat or gently undulating, the Germans use steel turrets because of the much lower silhouette of steel turrets as compared to concrete pillboxes.

e. Communications

The primary means of communication is a double cable system, which is buried deep in the earth so that it cannot be reached by the bombardment of attacking artillery and air forces. Of course, the Germans supplement their buried cable system with other means of communications, such as radio, messengers, etc.

The Germans fully appreciate the importance of maintaining communications and control within a fortified system in which the fires of many forts and emplacements must be coordinated. This was demonstrated when the disruption of French communications proved to be an important factor in the breaking of the Maginot Line. The French depended upon wire laid aboveground, a few radios, and messengers; when the Germans destroyed these facilities, the French forces lost coordination.

f. Gasproofing

The forts that have been described are to a great extent gasproof. The critical defending weapons can still fire through concentrations of gas, because they have gun shields which are made with fairly close tolerances. Rubber gaskets at the points of contact of metal on metal improve the sealing of these gun shields. Gas blowers operated by machinery purify contaminated air drawn from the outside and maintain pure air within the forts at pressures slightly greater than atmospheric; thus all leakages will be of pure inside air to the outside. Manually operated purifying units are ready in case of power failure.

g. Power Installations

The power units for West Wall installations are believed to be complete within each group of forts. The Germans do not rely on any single, indispensable cable to bring in electric power from some plant in the rear. The German aim is to make these installations as self-sufficient as possible. Batteries are maintained as available replacement of the built-in sources of power which are necessary for water pumps, operation of gasproofing machinery, electricity, cooking, underground railway operations, elevators for ammunition supply, etc.

21. CLOSED FORTIFICATIONS

Information is available on an installation of the closed type on the Polish border, and it may be assumed that those of this type in the West Wall have similar characteristics. The underground shelters of the installation provided quarters for two infantry regiments (6,000 men), whose mission was to cover a front of 4,000 yards. In the design of the works complete familiarity with possible developments in the tactical situation were contemplated. The terrain had been analyzed to determine the probable methods of attacks, and plans were drawn to circumvent any success of the attacker. This installation had 36 exits of the type illustrated in figure 22. Thus, at the proper moment for counterattack, the troops could debouch rapidly and put into effect previously prepared plan A, B, or C, depending on the situation.

The multiplicity of exits in such an installation allows tactical mobility on the battlefield without unnecessary exposure. Troops are committed fresh, as a unit, without casualties and without having had to endure the moral strain of hostile artillery fire while waiting to attack.

Figure 23 indicates the compactness and completeness of the underground living quarters. The photograph shows the special steel-spring beds hinged to

Figure 22.—Surface exit of closed shelter. (Note the sectionalized wooden trapdoor.)

Figure 23.—Sleeping quarters in the West Wall. (Note the special steel beds, electric lights, lavatories, and running water taps.)

the walls, the electric lighting, the wall lockers, and the lavatories with running water.

22. TYPICAL WORKS ON THE RHINE

Figures 24 through 31 are photographs of typical fortifications in the Rhine Line, in various degrees of completion.

23. CAMOUFLAGE

In the development of their fortified zones, the Germans rate camouflage as equal in importance to the thickness of concrete walls. Every effort is made to preserve the natural appearance of the ground from the moment construction is begun. Where the original conformation of the ground is broken by the unnatural lines of permanent construction, the structure is blended into the ground by means of garnished flat-tops, shrubbery, paint, or directly applied texture reproductions.

Flat-tops are commonly used over entrances to fortifications (fig. 32, p. 92, below). Supports of strong galvanized iron wire or chicken mesh are garnished with dyed burlap in irregular patches, covering about one-half of the flat-top area.

The exposed concrete and steel surfaces are generally covered with a material resembling coarse excelsior which has been dipped in glue or colored cement and then plastered against the exposed portions of the works. The hardened material is tough and difficult to remove, and not only breaks the reflection of light from flat surfaces, but approximates the color and texture of the surrounding terrain. Sod and

①

②

Figure 24.—Work with cupola, in course of embanking.

①

②

Figure 25.—Double flanking casemate, with wing-walls.

Figure 26.—Work with cupola, embanked.

Figure 27.—Double flanking casemate.

Figure 28.—Frontal casemate with embrasure.

Figure 29.—Work with cupola, reinforced by sheet piling.

Figure 30.—Embrasure covering rear of firing chamber.

Figure 31.—Embrasure for defense of entrances.

Figure 32.—Flat-top camouflage over entrance.

Figure 33.—Camouflage of concrete surface.

shrubbery are carefully replaced over shelters cut into
the earth, and are often supplemented by hay and
dried grass (fig. 33).

Landscapers who follow construction crews replace
original vegetation and, where necessary, plant additional shrubs to camouflage entrances and firing ports.
Camoufleurs and crews aid in maintaining a natural
cover over the fortifications (figs. 34 and 35). By
using live vegetation such as grass, shrubbery, trees,
and vines the camouflage is made both easier to maintain and more effective. The landscaping is, of course,
designed so as to avoid having the vegetation emphasize
the outlines of the fortifications.

Figure 34.——Camouflaged shelter.

Figure 35.—Camouflaging a machine-gun nest.

Figure 36 is an illustration of disruptive painting applied to a closed infantry shelter.

24. FIELD FORTIFICATIONS

a. General

The offensive nature of German permanent fortifications is emphasized by the thorough manner in which they are supplemented by field fortifications. Such field works are interspersed liberally throughout the West Wall. They cover dead areas, if any, with small-arms fire, and they enhance the strength of the

Figure 36.—Bunker camouflaged by disruptive painting.

permanent fortifications by making it possible to engage the enemy before he approaches close enough to
carry out close reconnaissance, direct fire, or demoli-
tions against the main works.

The most important functions of these field fortifications is to facilitate the counterattack and to lend
mobility to the defense. By strengthening even the
slightest advantageous feature of the ground they
become in effect the flexible lines of the immovable
forts. They are designed with the idea of projecting
forward the most vital element in warfare, the fighting
man. German doctrine stresses the human element
rather than artificial works. In other words, the
concrete does not exist to protect the soldier. Its

primary function is to insure uninterrupted fire by the defensive weapons in the fortified works. The psychological effect of this emphasis on the soldier is to make him appreciate that the Army relies chiefly on him for success in defense.

b. Construction

Basic principles for the design and construction of field fortifications are prescribed in the German manual *Infantry Field Fortifications (Feldbefestigung der Infanterie).* It may be assumed that these principles were followed in building the field works which complement the permanent works of the West Wall. The discussion quoted below is taken from this manual.

"Installations are marked out and built only after the location of emplacements and direction of fire have been determined from the fire plan. The time required for construction is calculated in advance. It is better to set up a few well-camouflaged, finished emplacements than to have many half-finished emplacements. The type of design of the emplacement is determined primarily by the working time available. Ground conditions, drainage, weather, possibilities of concealment, and availability of labor effectives, entrenching tools, and other construction tools and materials must be taken into consideration. In the vicinity of the enemy, defense must always be possible during construction.

"Emplacements must be adapted to the terrain in order to make broad use of natural concealment. To provide maximum protection against high-trajectory weapons, the works must be built as small as possible, consistent with effectiveness. Field works should be sloped to the extent necessary to keep them from caving in. Revetting of the walls of excavations may be necessary in loose earth and in emplacement construction on stabilized fronts. The debris resulting from gunfire on revetments made of heavy material is difficult to clear away. Therefore, revetments built of such material should have broader bases than usual.

"The earth initially excavated for field works must be carried far enough away to make a second shifting of it unnecessary. Excavated earth must be dumped inconspicuously some distance from the installations. The routes for carrying away the earth must be closely regulated. If the situation and enemy action permit, turf should be cut out of the area that will be filled in with spoil. The cut grass is later used for camouflaging installations.

"Parapets should be extended far enough around the sides of emplacements to enable gunners to fire in all directions, and to protect them against enemy flanking fire. Parapets should be kept low, but the field of fire must not be masked by the growth of vegetation.

"The dimensions given in the examples of field fortifications are only suggestions. The works must be adapted to the individual sizes of the men. As an aid in measuring installations, the spade length should be used. The short spade is 50 cm (20 inches), the long spade 110 cm (43 inches). The length of the blade of the spade is about 20 cm (8 inches).

"In terrain that is difficult to camouflage because it is flat, or uniform in hue, it may be preferable to

avoid excavations for certain works: for example, emplacements for silent weapons. In such a case platforms or supports for the weapons are installed on the
surface of the ground, provided that the weapons can
be so situated that they do not make too high a
silhouette.

"*Camouflage during construction.*—It is not possible
to provide concealment against enemy flyers for all
emplacement construction. However, steps must be
taken to prevent individual installations, especially
heavy machine-gun emplacements, observation posts,
and shelters, from appearing clearly in aerial photographs. Sites with natural camouflage and concealment are especially well suited for emplacements.

"In laying out a position, care must be taken to
make sure that the installations cause as little change
as possible in the appearance of the ground, and that
they do not unnaturally interrupt the characteristic
lines of the terrain. Trees and shrubbery within the
emplacement area should be removed only from specially designated sites. In clearing a field of fire, the
opening in the vegetation must be made carefully.
The best method is to loop branches and remove
undergrowth and shrubbery.

"Car and wagon tracks and trampled paths leading
away from roads should not run directly to the installations and end there, but should terminate beyond
them, or continue on as dummy roads to some existing
true road or into woods. Access to the installations
proper should be by short spur trails, and they must
be constantly effaced by raking or by being covered
with straw.

"Construction materials should be delivered in single vehicles, not in convoys, preferably during darkness, and they must always follow prescribed routes. Such materials and equipment must be stored under trees and shrubbery or at the base of ridges, in which case they should be covered with branches or camouflage netting.

"*Camouflage of finished installations.*—The camouflage of installations must approximate the color and texture of the surrounding terrain. Branches and sod must not be removed from the immediate vicinity, and traces of work must be effaced. Left-over construction material and equipment must be taken away. Sharp edges and angles must always be avoided. The shadows of entrances, foxholes, and trenches are camouflaged with netting. Communication trenches should be camouflaged with vegetation.

"To minimize the danger of enemy surface observation on frontal terrain, field works, especially those for machine guns and riflemen, should have background cover that will blur out silhouettes. Shrubbery and undulations of the terrain are proper backgrounds. When construction has been completed, the efficacy of these backgrounds must be checked from the direction of the enemy.

"Camouflage must not interfere with our own firing, and it must not be necessary to remove the camouflage in order to fire. Camouflage nets must not be revealed by their shadows, and, therefore, in broken terrain they should be somewhat arched; in flat terrain the nets should be stretched flat. If there is no overlap with natural lines of the terrain, such as hedges, roads, and ridges, the edges of camouflage covers must be made irregular. In winter, camouflage nets must be well-braced against the weight of snow.

"*Dummy installations.*—The execution of dummy installations requires much understanding and skill. Company and battalion commanders must carefully integrate dummy installations into the defense plan. Knee-deep excavations are sufficient for dummy works. The sides should be cut steep and the bottoms covered with dark brushwood. In spite of camouflage, the installation must be recognizable through seeming carelessness, such as by trampled paths and gaps in the camouflage.

"In barren areas it may be advisable to place many heaps of earth or refuse to divert the enemy from genuine installations. Dummy installations must seem to be occupied. Therefore from time to time they should be actually occupied and rifle and heavy gun fire delivered from them. The dummy works must be so designed that troops temporarily occupying them may leave without attracting the attention of the enemy."

c. Examples of Field Fortifications

All of the photographs and sketches (figs. 37 through 48) included under this heading have also been taken from the German manual *Infantry Field Fortifications*. The manual is dated 15 January 1940. It is realized that the Germans have undoubtedly revised their field-fortification technique in the light of recent combat experience. However, it is believed that the illustrations are still useful to demonstrate basic German practice.

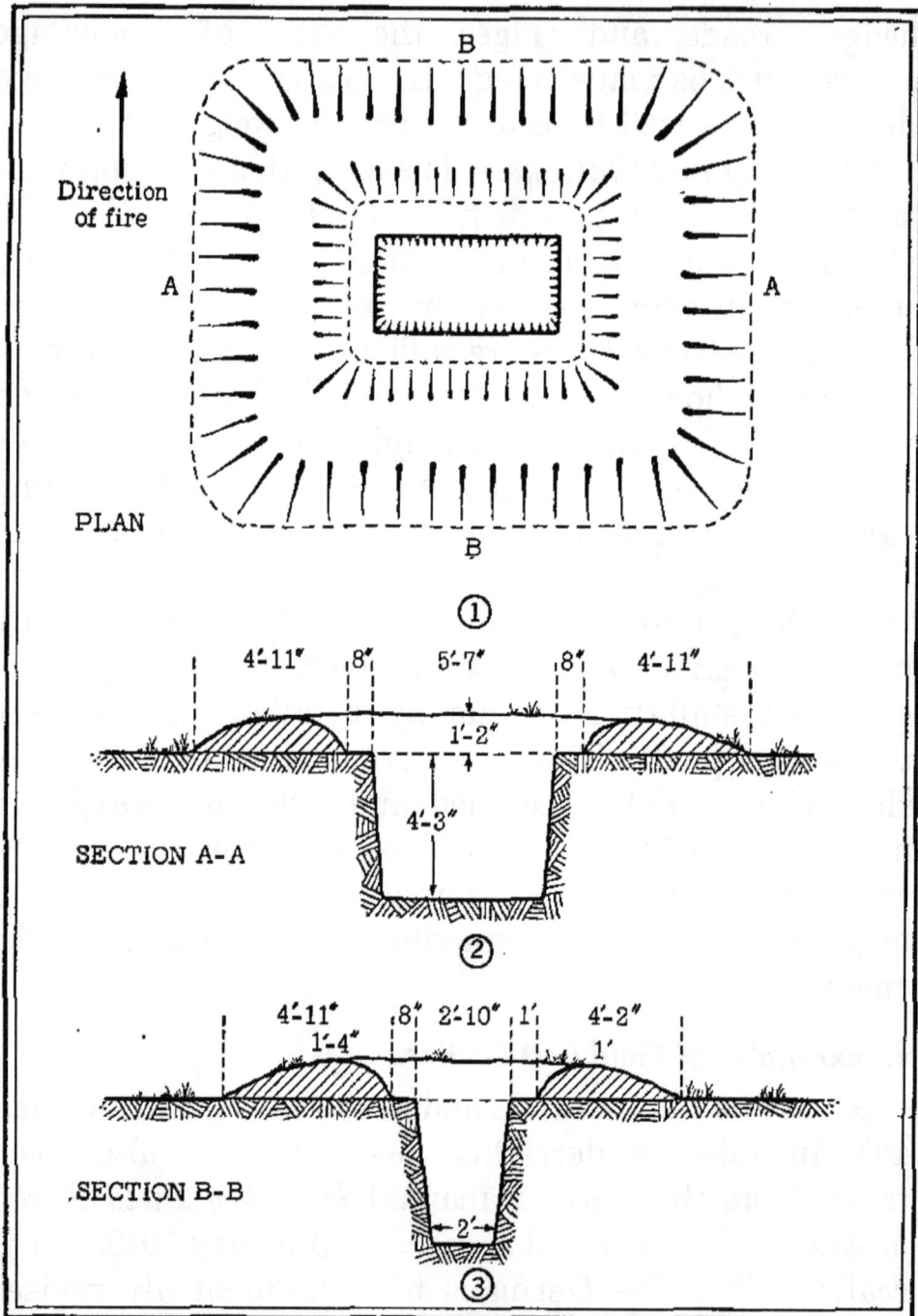

Figure 37.—Riflemen's foxhole for two gunners.

Suggested improvements:[2] Lengthening the foxhole on both sides and adding sitting ledges; a drainage sump with duckboard; ammunition niches.

[2] The suggested improvements and other comments are quoted from the German manual.

①

Figure 38.—Foxhole for light machine gun or antitank rifle.

Suggested improvements: Lengthening the foxhole on both sides and adding sitting ledges; a drainage sump with duckboard; ammunition niches.

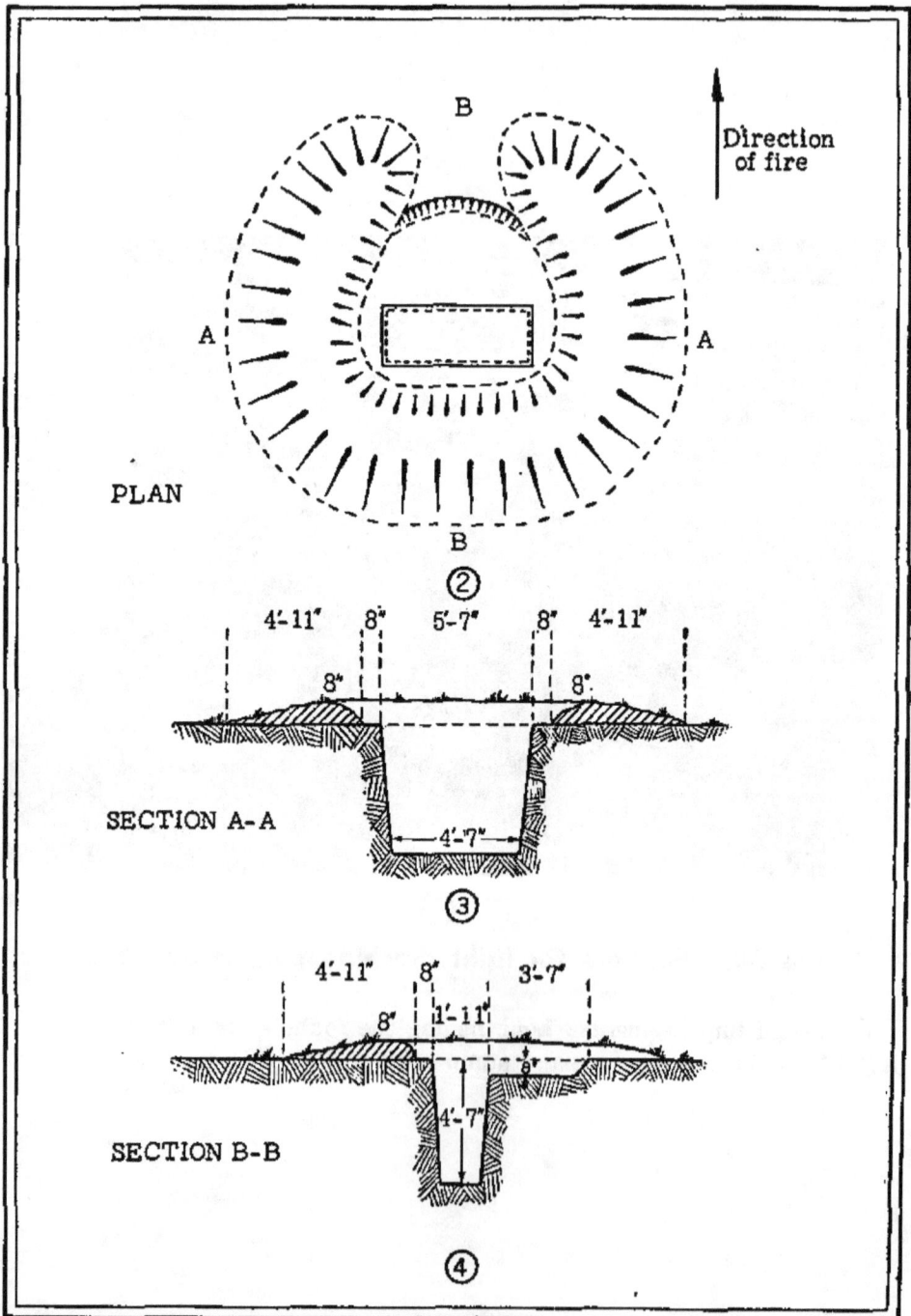

Figure 38 (continued).—Foxhole for light machine gun or antitank rifle.

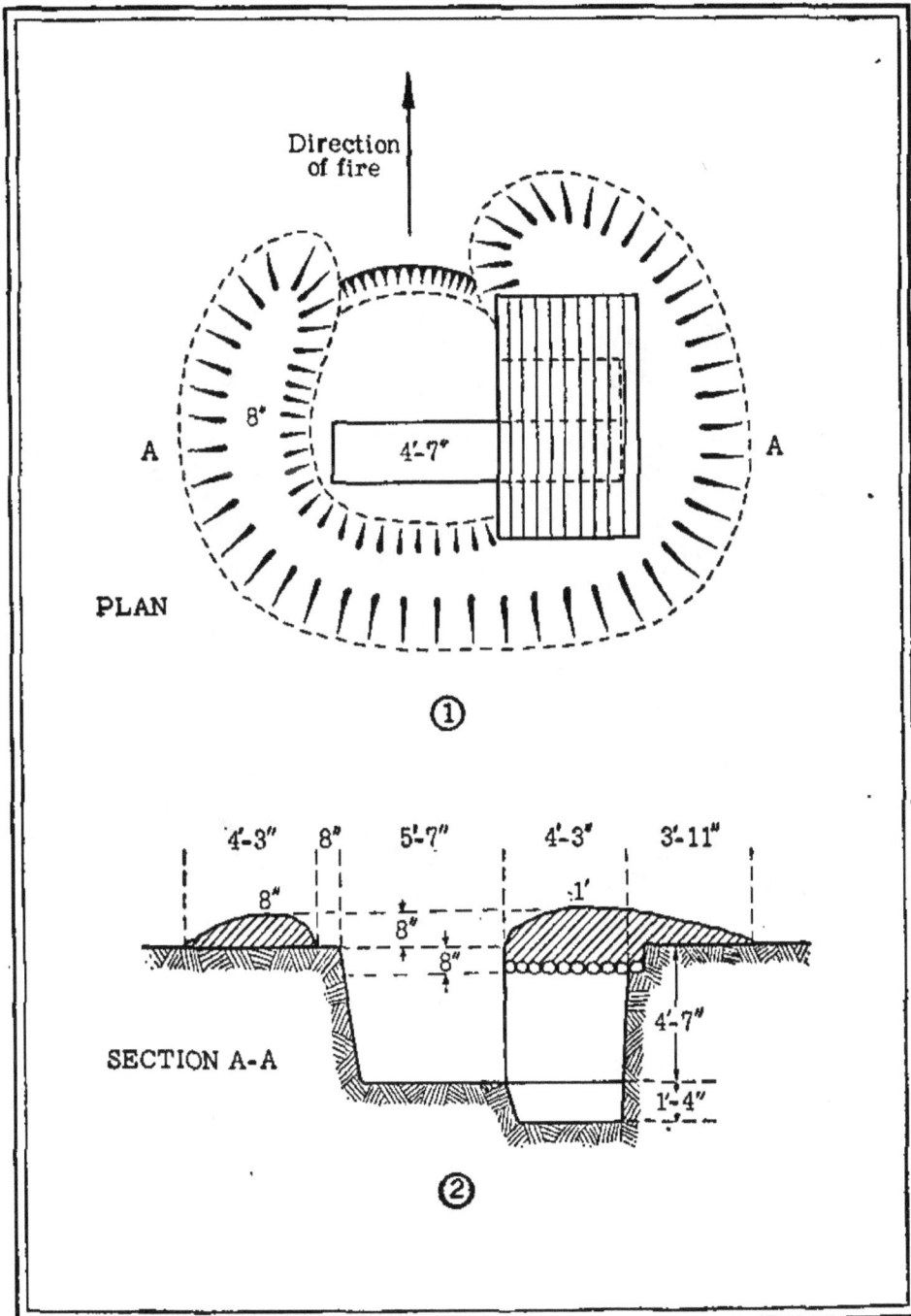

Figure 39.—Foxhole for light machine gun and dugout for three men.

Suggested improvements: Building a drainage sump with duckboard; building in munitions niches.

①

Figure 40.—Emplacement for light mortar.

The mortar base must be placed far enough forward to prevent earth loosened by blast from falling into the foxhole.

The base plate must be at least 8 inches from the edge of the cut.

Direction of fire

3'-7"   5'-7"

A   A

PLAN

②

Light mortar
support

10"   10"

1'-7"

4'-3"

SECTION A-A

10"   2'-4"   1'-6"   ⅔-2"

③

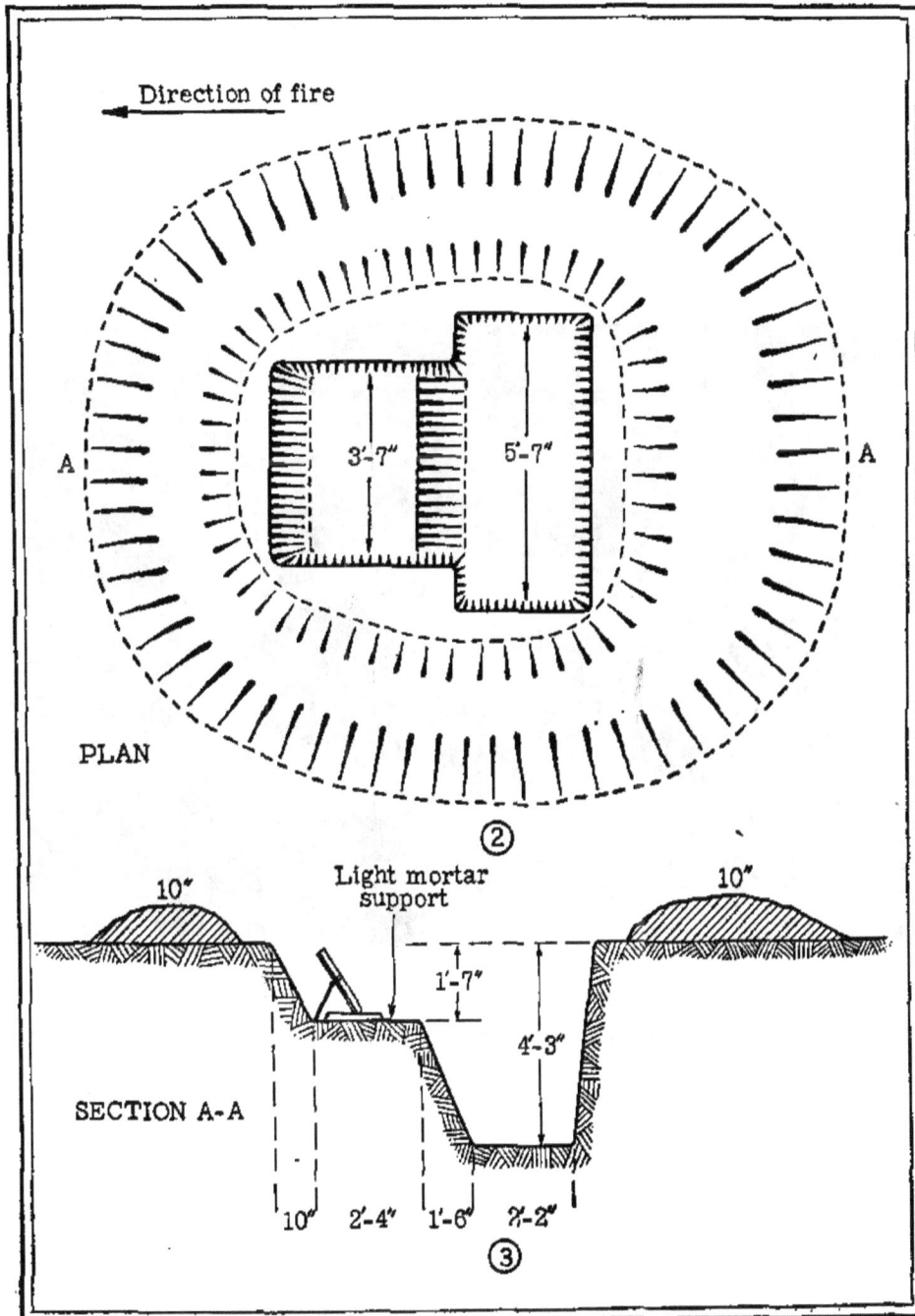

Figure 40 (continued).—Emplacement for light mortar.

Suggested improvements: Lengthening the foxhole on both sides and
adding sitting ledges; a drainage sump with duckboard.

①

Figure 41.—Enlarged foxhole for light mortar, with revetted slope.

Revetting the slope makes the manipulation of the light mortar easier.

Direction of fire

2'-11" 8'-2"

A ||— —|| A

PLAN

②

10"

2'-4" 1'-8"

Light mortar support

SECTION A-A

1'-8" 4'-7"

Planks

2'-2"

③

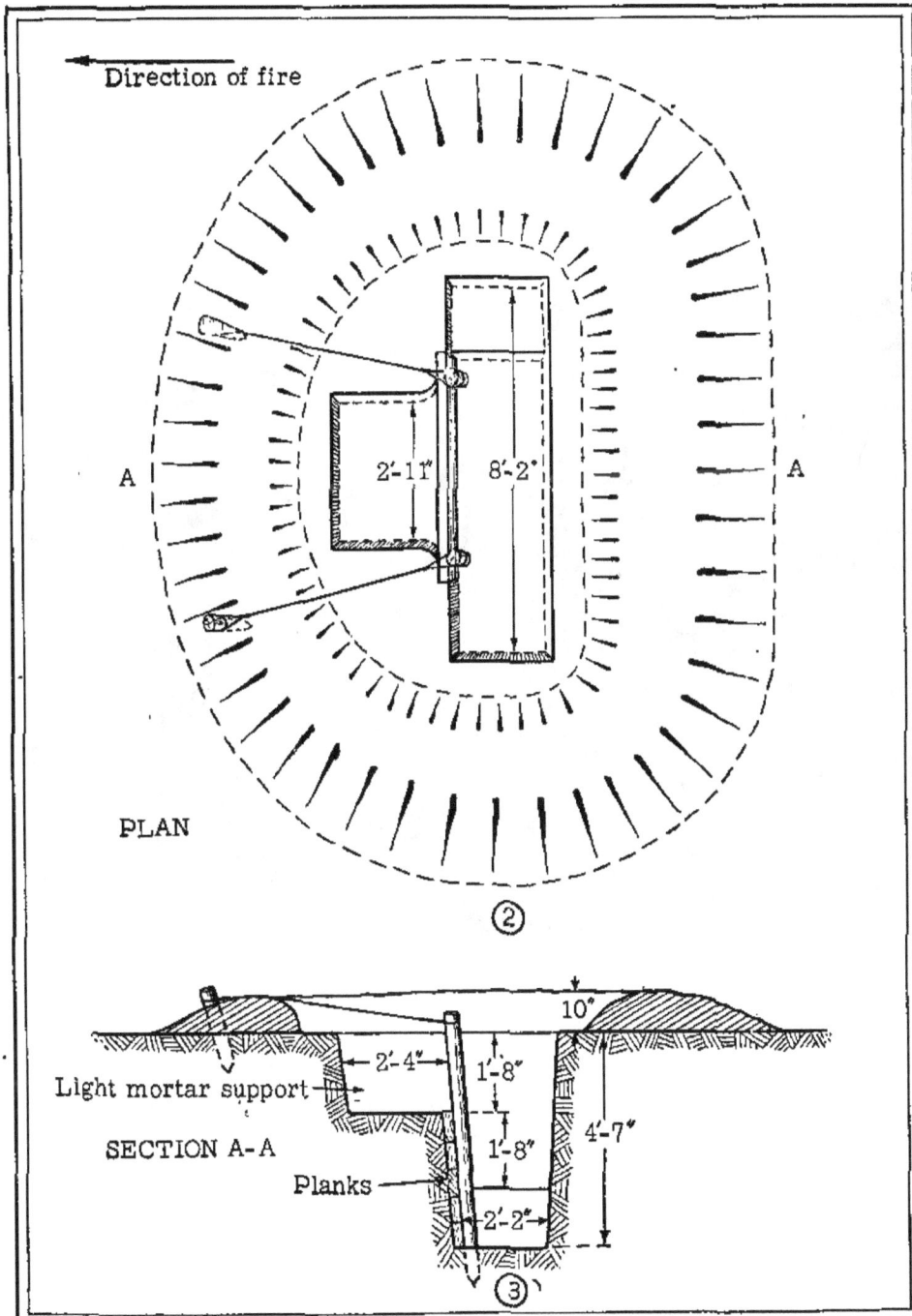

Figure 41 (continued).—Enlarged foxhole for light mortar, with revetted slope.

Construction materials for revetting the face:

    (a) 2 round posts 4 inches by 6   (c) 3 planks 2 by 12 by 60 inches
        feet 3 inches.

    (b) 2 round posts 4 inches by 2   (d) 33 feet of smooth wire.

①

Figure 42.—Foxhole for heavy machine gun and three men.

The walls are built at angles that will prevent a cave-in.

The two foxholes for the remainder of the machine-gun group are staggered at intervals of 15 to 25 feet to the side and rear.

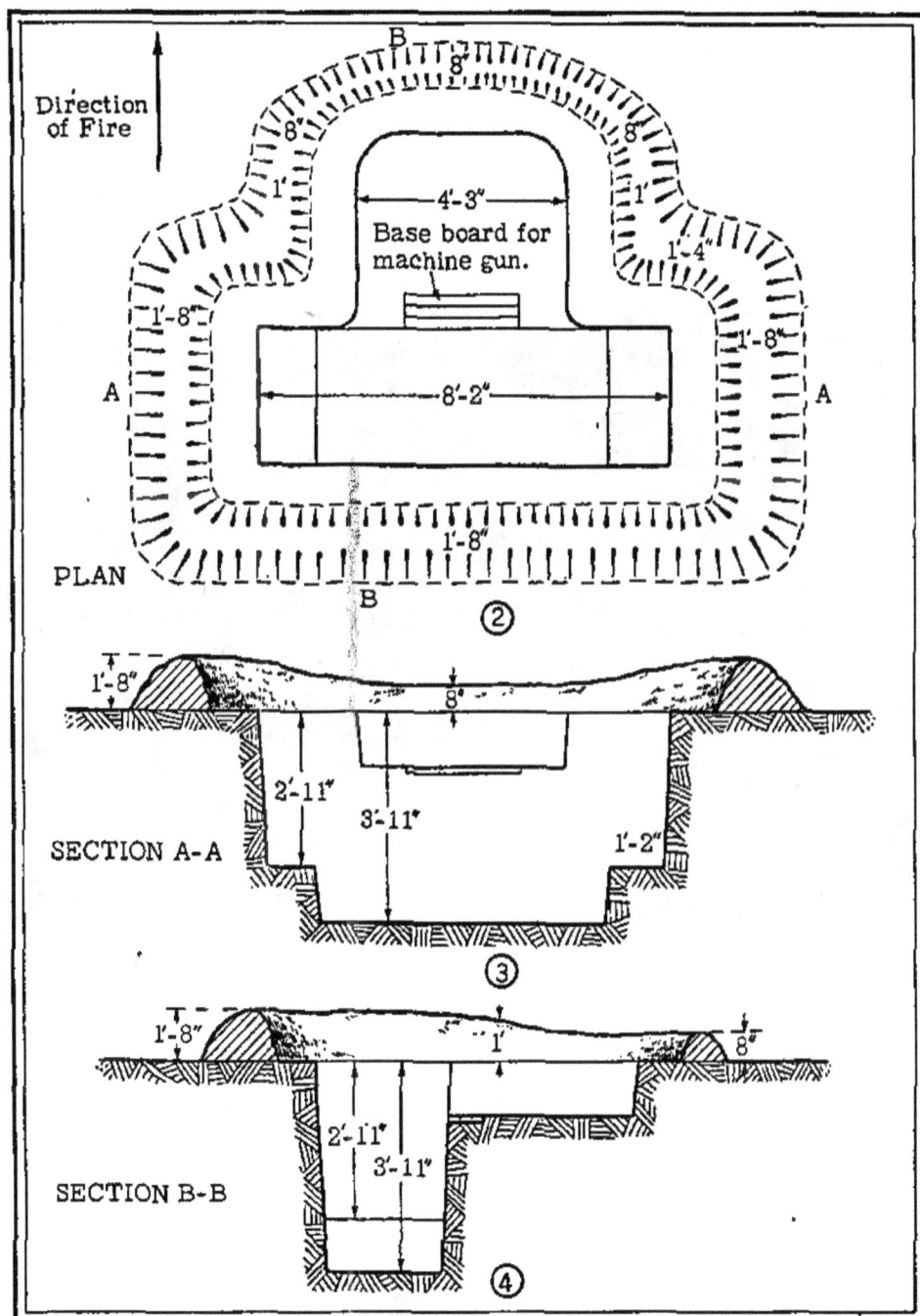

Figure 42 (continued).—Foxhole for heavy machine gun and three men.

The firing support is provided by cutting the machine-gun base into the ground; the depth of the foxhole is 5 feet; the height of the parados and lateral parapets, 12 inches; and the depth of the machine-gun base, 8 inches.

The installation often has no sitting ledges.

Figure 43.—Three-man foxhole for heavy machine gun, with dugout.

Suggested improvements: Building a drainage sump with duckboard; building in munitions niches.

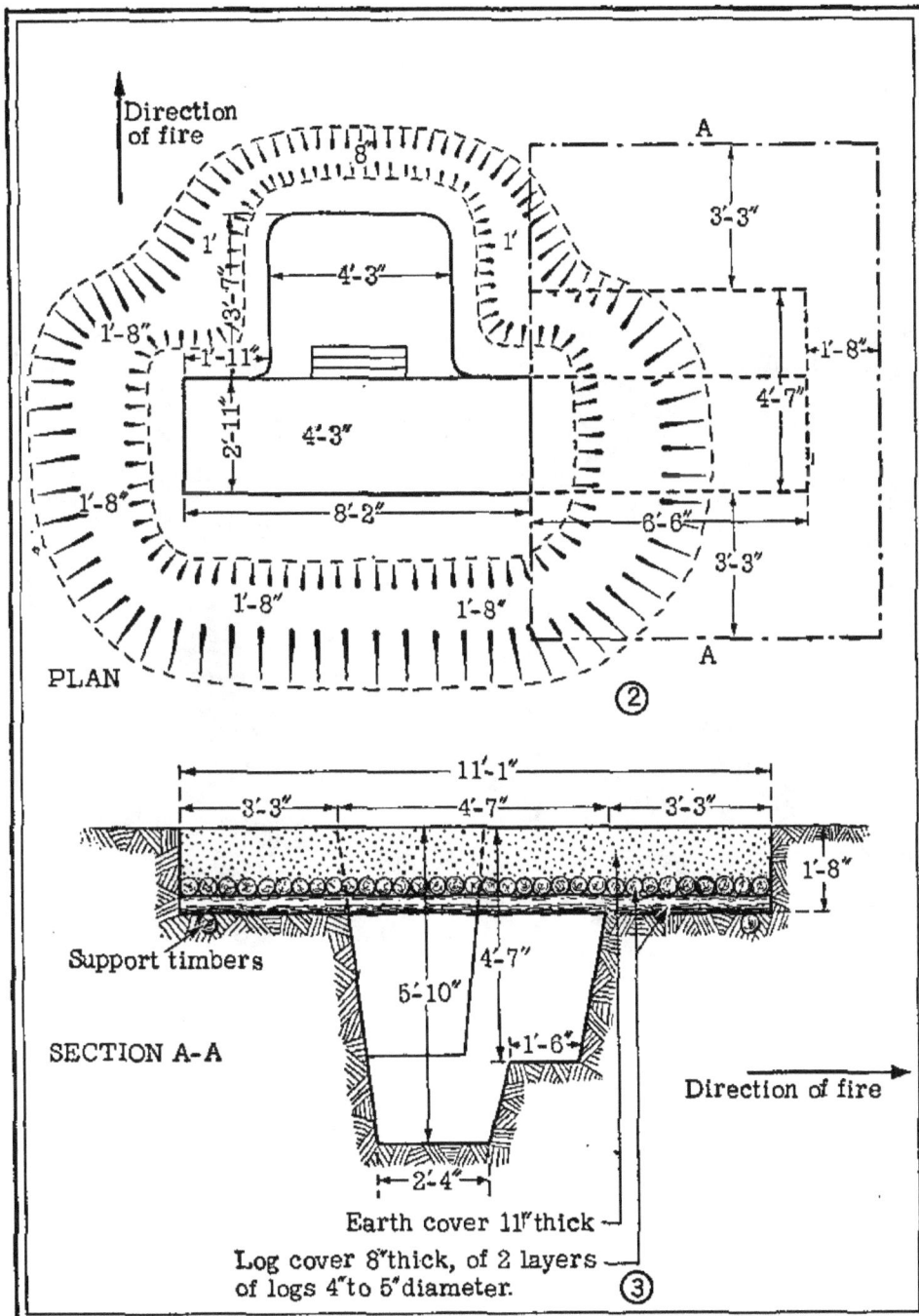

Figure 43 (continued).—Three-man foxhole for heavy machine gun, with dugout.

Construction materials:

    (a) 25 round timbers 4 inches by 11 feet 3 inches.

    (b) 26 round timbers 4 inches by 8 feet 3 inches.

①

Figure 44.—Heavy mortar emplacement.

For purposes of illustration, the camouflage of the foxhole and helmets has been omitted.

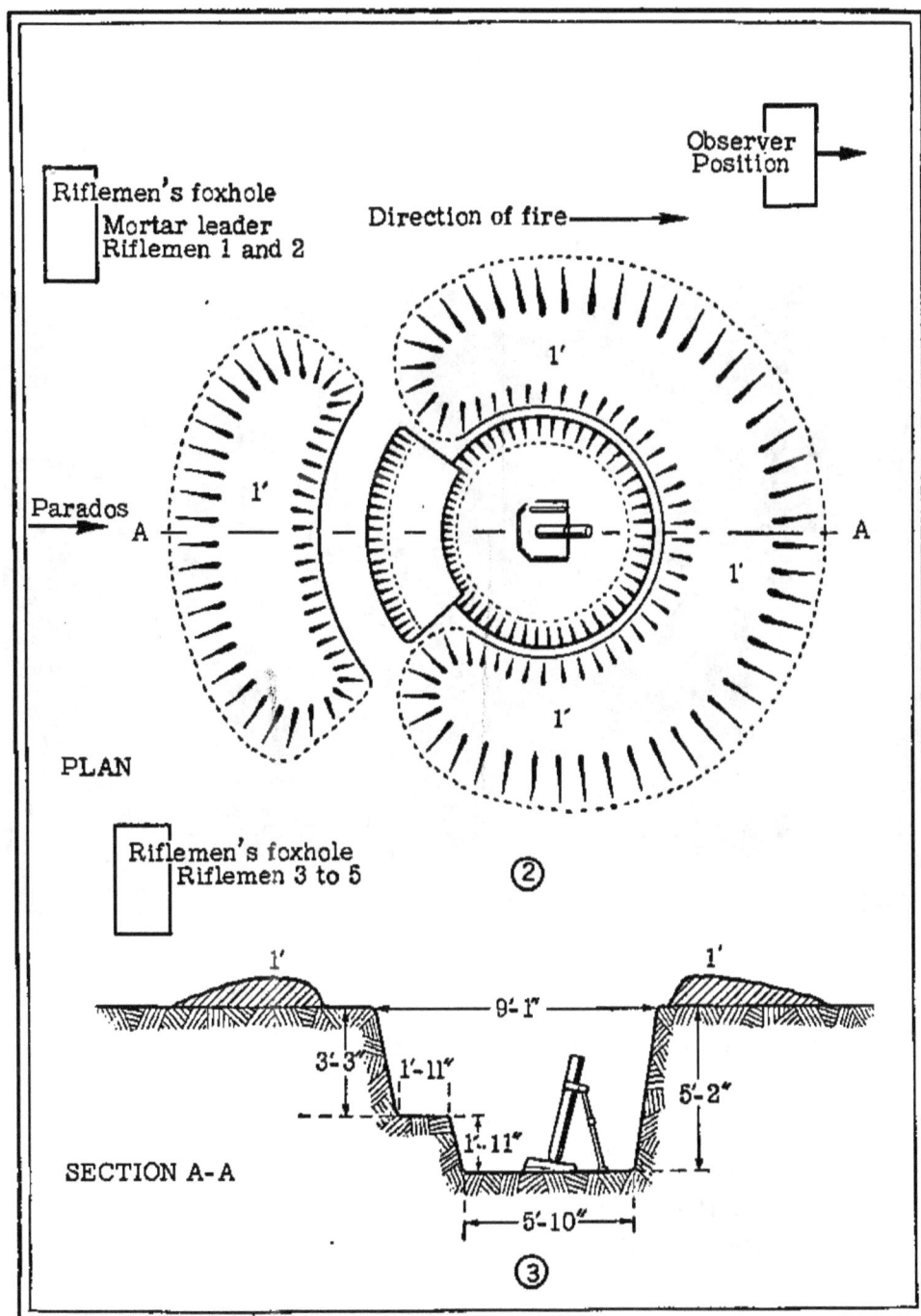

Riflemen's foxhole
Mortar leader
Riflemen 1 and 2

Direction of fire

Observer
Position

Parados

A

A

1'

1'

1'

1'

PLAN

Riflemen's foxhole
Riflemen 3 to 5

②

1'   1'

9'-1"

3'-3"   1'-11"

5'-2"

1'-11"

SECTION A-A

5'-10"

③

Figure 44 (continued).—Heavy mortar emplacement.

Sequence of construction:

    (a) Foxholes for the crew.

    (b) Installation for the heavy mortar.

Figure 45.—Emplacement for light infantry gun.

Building the installation for the light infantry gun takes six men 2 hours.

Nearby cover for the crew is prepared in advance.

Sequence of construction:

    (a) Foxholes for the crew.

    (b) Installation for the light infantry gun.

    (c) Ammunition pits.

Riflemen's foxhole

Gun leader and
riflemen 1 and 2

Direction of fire ⟶

Riflemen
5 and 6

Riflemen
3 and 4

Munitions 3'-11"
3'-7"

Munitions 3'-3"
1'-11"

A

8"
45° 45°

PLAN

1'-11"
1'-11"

8'-6"

Exit

Entrance

Parados
1'-11"
3'-3"

A

②

8"
1'-11"

③

19'-9"

1'-11"
3'-3"

SECTION A-A

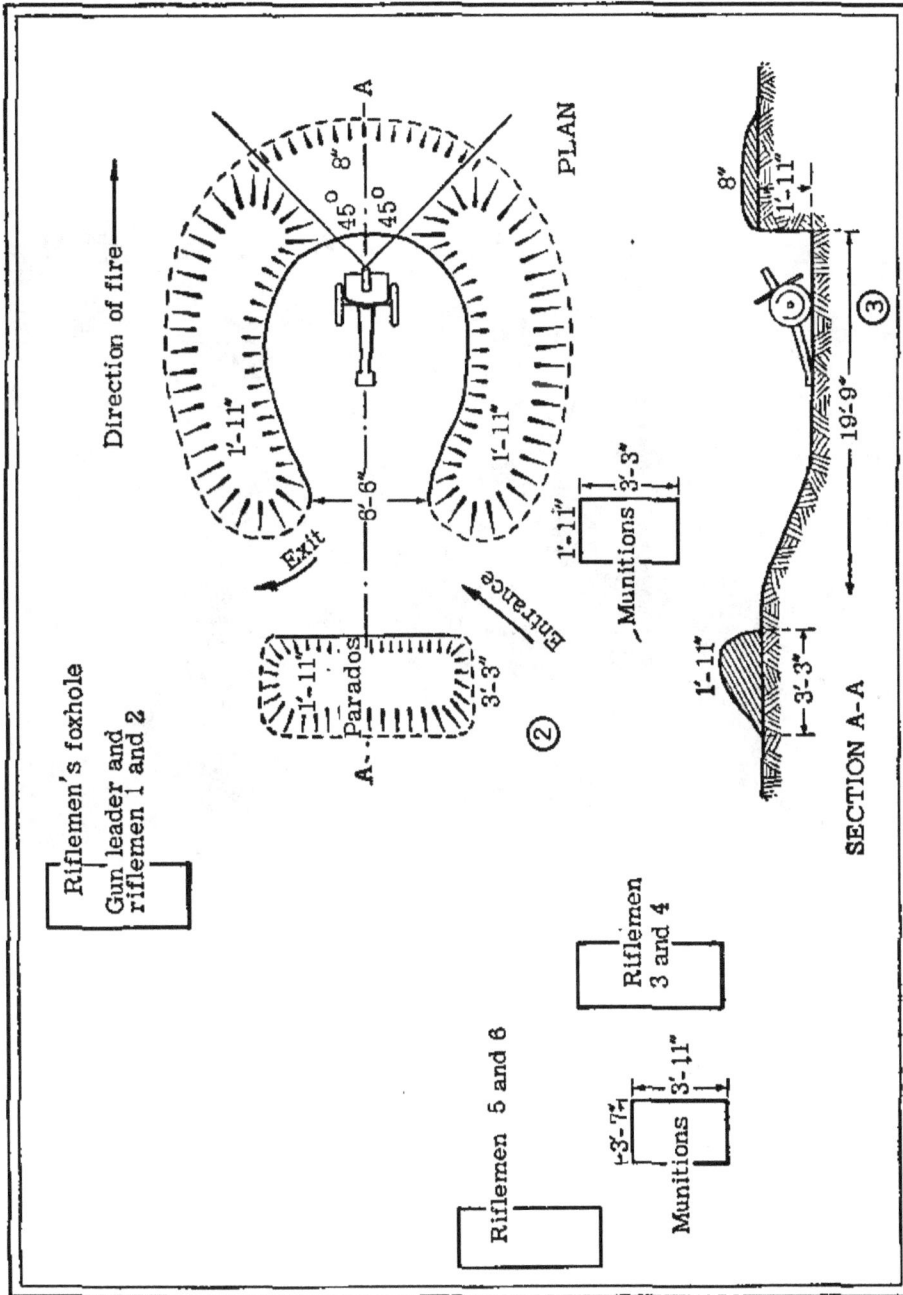

Figure 45 (*continued*).—Emplacement for light infantry gun.

①

Figure 46.—Emplacement for antitank gun in flat terrain.

The height of the parados is dependent on the base clearance of the gun.

Sequence of construction:
(a) Firing emplacement for the gun.
(b) Cover for the crew.

Riflemen's foxhole

1'-11" 1'-8"

Munitions

Direction of fire

1'-6"

1'-4"

8"

Entrance

A Parados

12'-10"

A

8"

1'-6"

②

1'-8" 1'-11"

Munitions

PLAN Riflemen's foxhole

10"

2'-9"

1'-4"

SECTION A-A 15'-9"

③

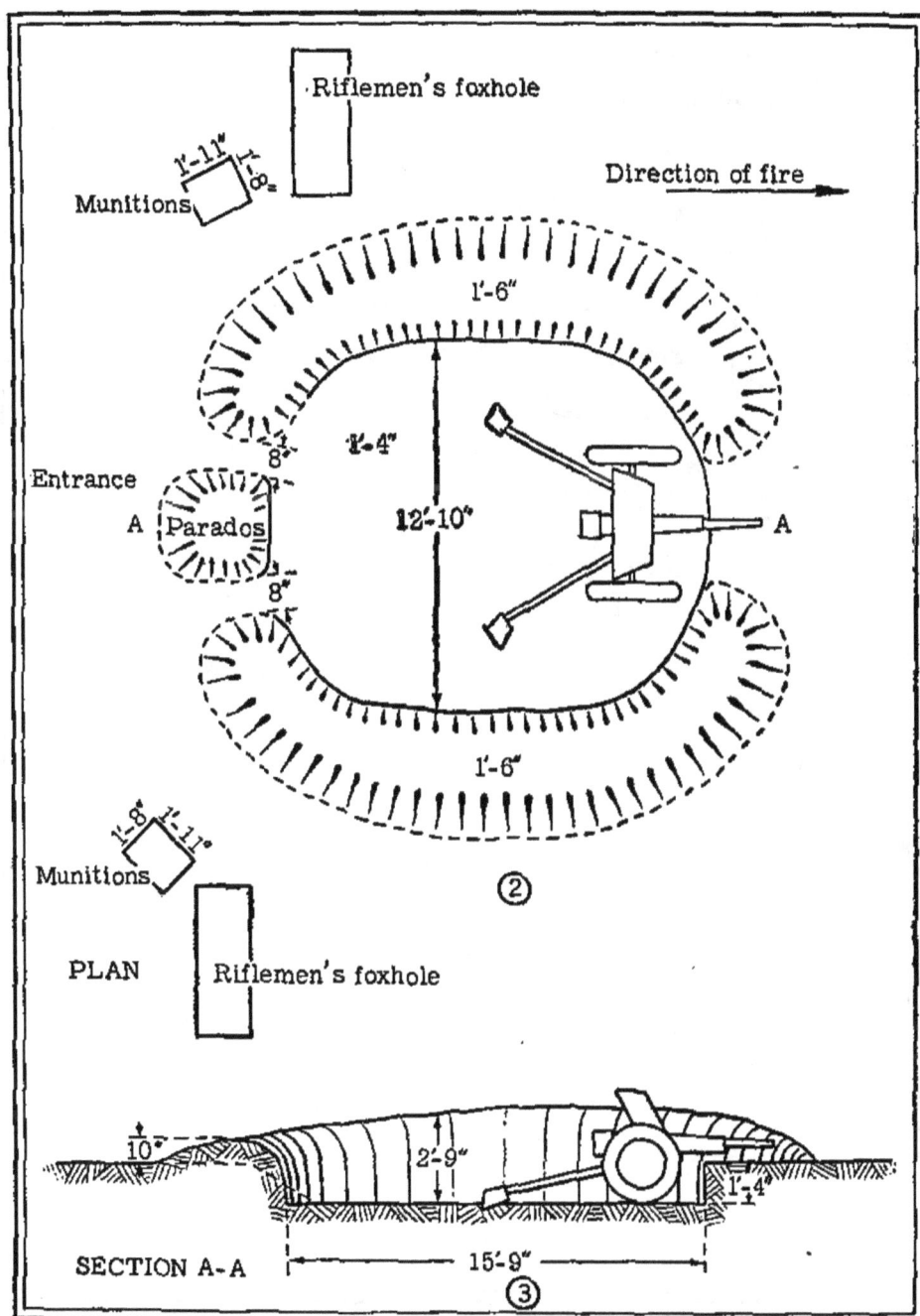

Figure 46 (continued).—Emplacement for antitank gun in flat terrain.

547714°—43——9

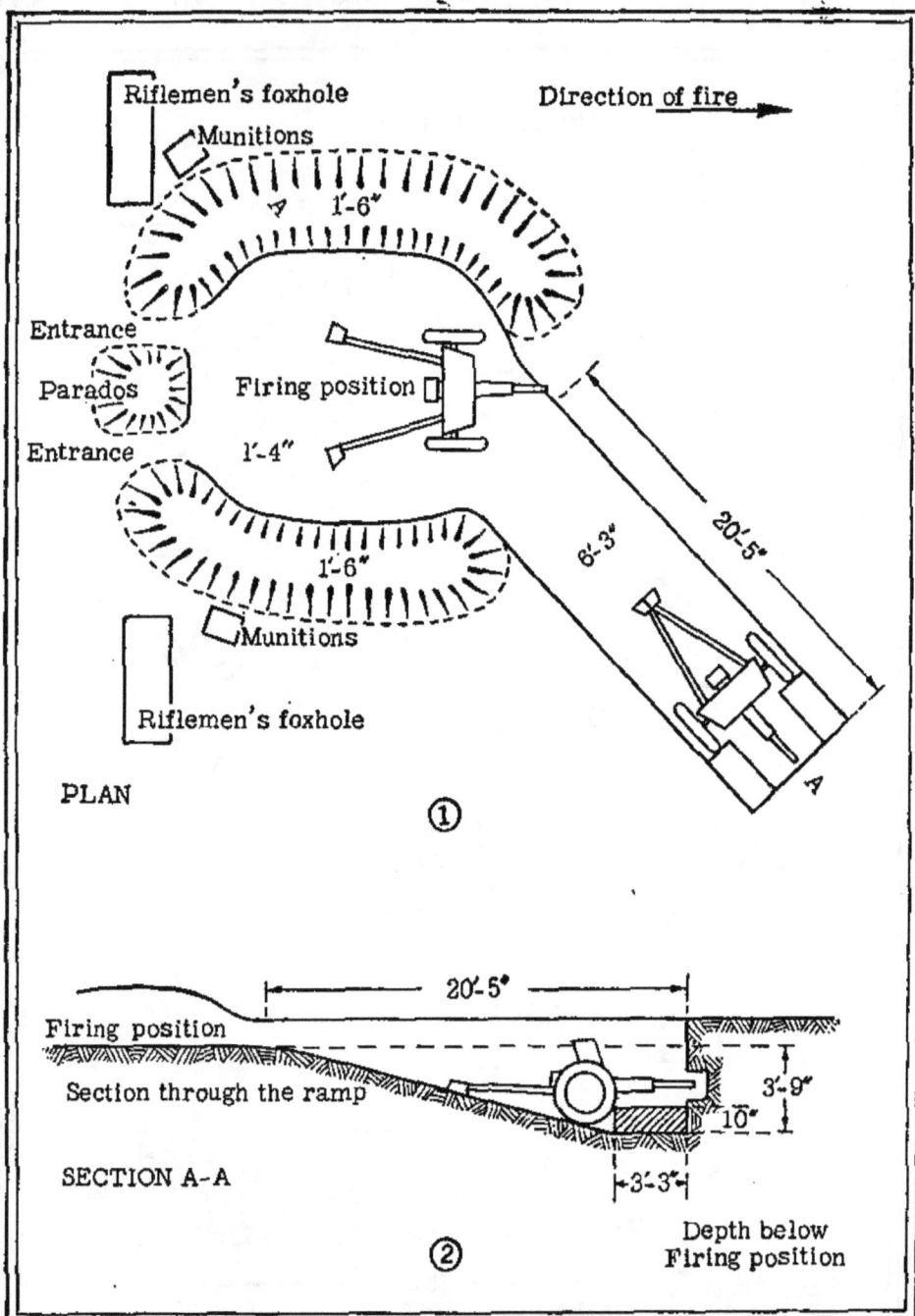

Figure 47.—Emplacement for antitank gun, with ramp.

The ramp is built at an angle of 45° from the principal direction of fire in order to prevent damage to the ramp by blast. The design is such that the antitank gun can be hauled backward into the firing position on the ramp, and removed from sight after fire.

③

Figure 47 (continued).—Emplacement for antitank gun, with ramp.

Construction materials:

      (a) 12 round timbers 3 inches by 2 feet 6 inches.

      (b) 45 round timbers 3 inches by 7 feet.

      (c) 7 planks 2 by 12 inches by 2 feet 6 inches.

      (d) 7 planks 2 by 12 inches by 7 feet.

      (e) 19 yards of wire mesh.

Earth removal: 26 cubic yards.

Legend

Ö No 1 gunner on light machine gun

Ö No 2 gunner on light machine gun

● Squad Leader

Ö No 3 gunner on light machine gun

◑ Assistant squad leader

○ Rifleman

Direction of fire →

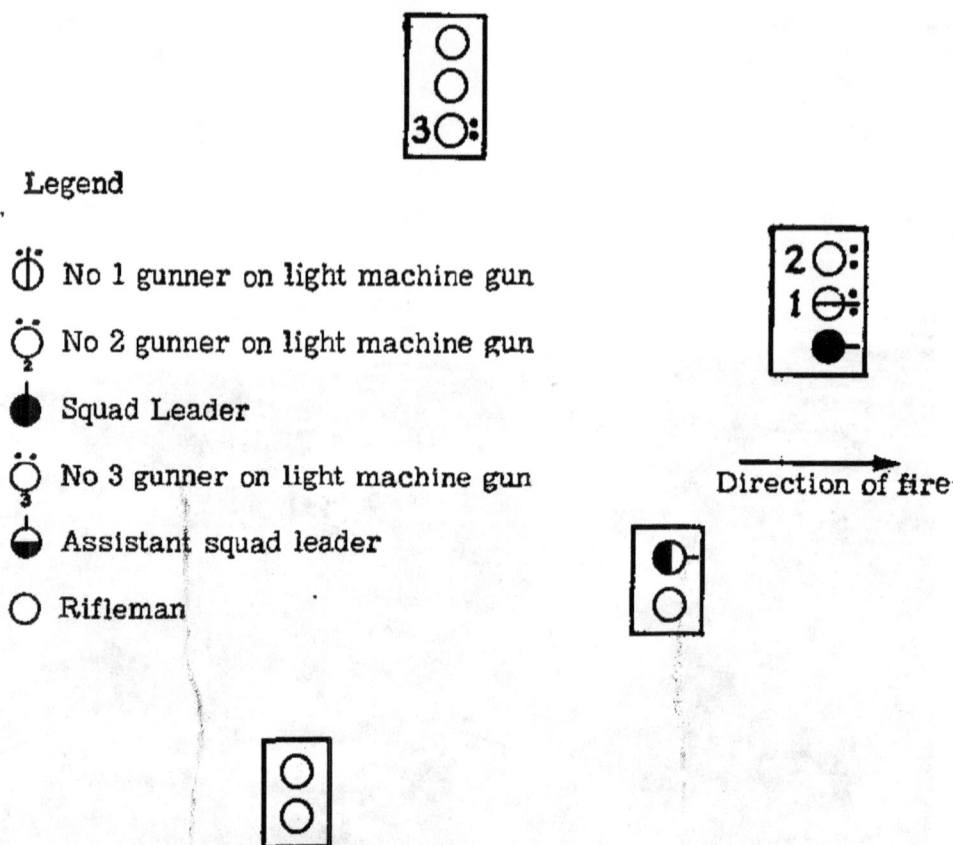

Figure 48.—Group of riflemen's foxholes.

The required width of the position is not more than 33 yards, with 4 to 9 yards between foxholes. The distribution in depth must be irregular in order to reduce the possibility of one shell making hits on more than one foxhole.

The squad leader must be able to maintain contact with all riflemen.

25. GUN EMPLACEMENTS

A majority of the emplacements for artillery and antiaircraft guns in the West Wall are of the open type. The German theory of the use of artillery requires mobility as an essential element of defense, and open emplacements allow the necessary degree of mobility within a system of permanent fortifications. Units of the field army that move into the fortified zones emplace their weapons in prepared positions—

in the permanent works as well as in the field fortifications. Certain batteries in critical positions are permanently emplaced behind concrete cover, but by far the greater part of the defending artillery is in the open and thus subject to counterbattery fire. Cover exists for the gun crews and for the ammunition supply, of which a permanent store is maintained, although the guns themselves may be moved frequently. Underground tunnels and signal communications have been installed for use by forward observers and by personnel moving to and from their positions. Defiladed and camouflaged roads also provide access to positions.

German artillery positions generally include one or more of the following types of installations:[3]

(a) Artillery observation posts.

(b) Bombproof ammunition storage shelters.

(c) Bombproof gun shelters and loophole emplacements.

(d) Double gun emplacements with one or more six-loophole turrets.

(e) Open gun emplacements with bombproof shelters for ammunition and crews.

Figure 49, based on sketches in *Die Ständige Front*, illustrates a German cover trench for artillery gun crews. The German manual recommends the employment of splinterproof roofs, made of wood, over these trenches to serve as camouflage, as well as protection against shell fragments. The dimensions in the illustration are intended for guidance only, the German

---

[3] The critically important emplacements are heavily constructed to form armored battery positions.

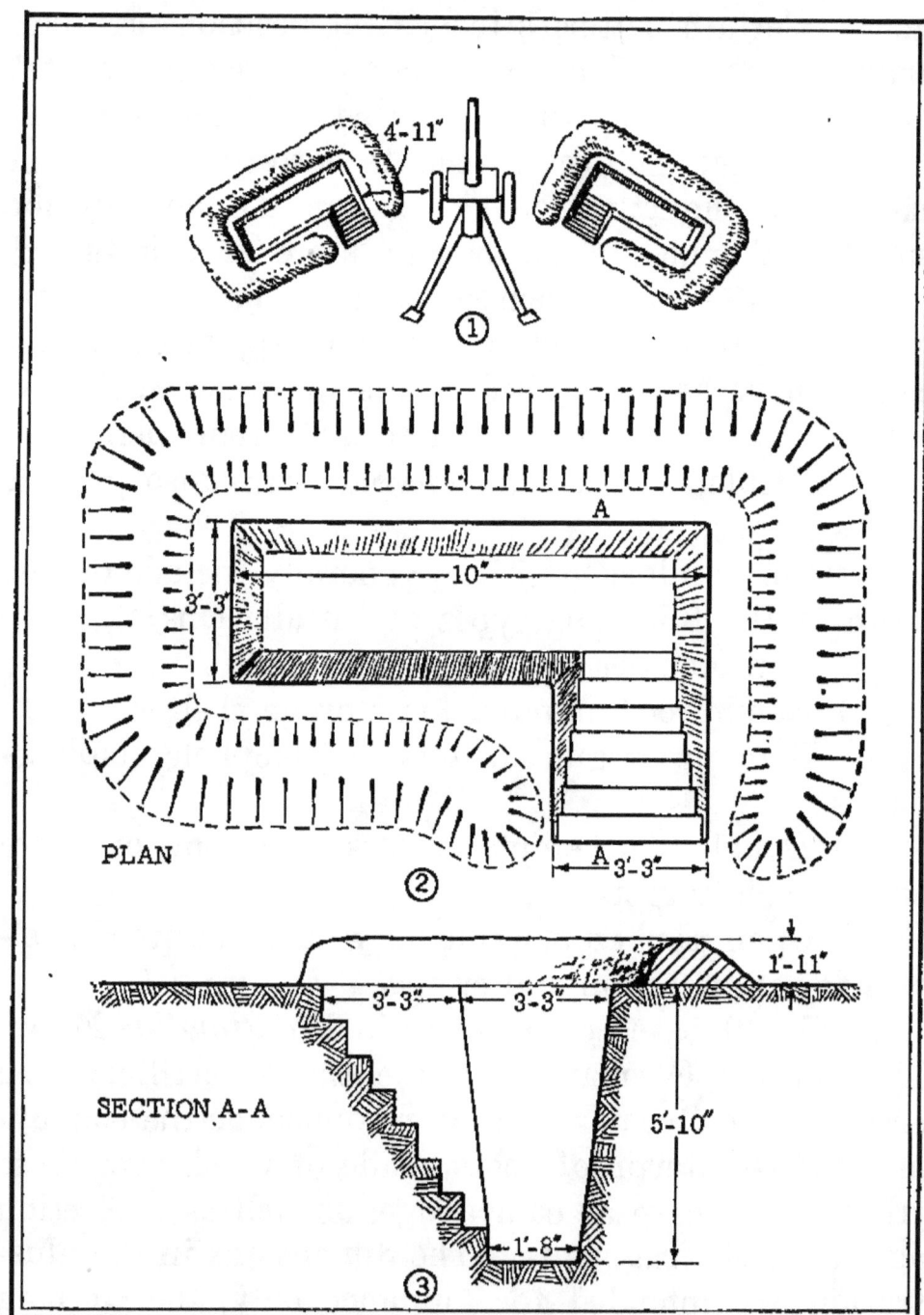

Figure 49.—Cover trench for gun crews.

manual prescribing that the trenches be dug as narrow and deep as the ground permits. For determining the length of the cover trench, the manual recommends a basic allowance of about one-half meter (20 inches) for each member of the crew. As indicated in figure 49 ①, the rear edge of the trench is laid out to point in the direction of the gun-wheel hub.

In the same manual are illustrated an open emplacement for a light or medium howitzer, or a 105-mm gun (fig. 50), and a sketch for an underground crew shelter (fig. 51). (The smaller dimensions in parentheses in figure 50 ① are for a light field howitzer emplacement.)

26. INSTALLATIONS OF THE AIR DEFENSE ZONE

a. General

In the air defense zone, antiaircraft gun and searchlight batteries are laid out in depth and staggered in order that their firing ranges will overlap. In sectors that have particularly important installations, the defenses are supplemented by balloon and kite barrage formations (*Luftsperrverbände*). Antiaircraft batteries are motorized, as well as being sited in permanent positions, and many new roads have been constructed in the zone to enable the rapid concentration of antiaircraft guns for the protection of heavily attacked targets. Within the zone is an aircraft warning service with its own telephone and radio communication system for warning ground defenses and fighter squadrons.

Emplacements in the zone are of the permanent and field fortification types. They vary in size and con-

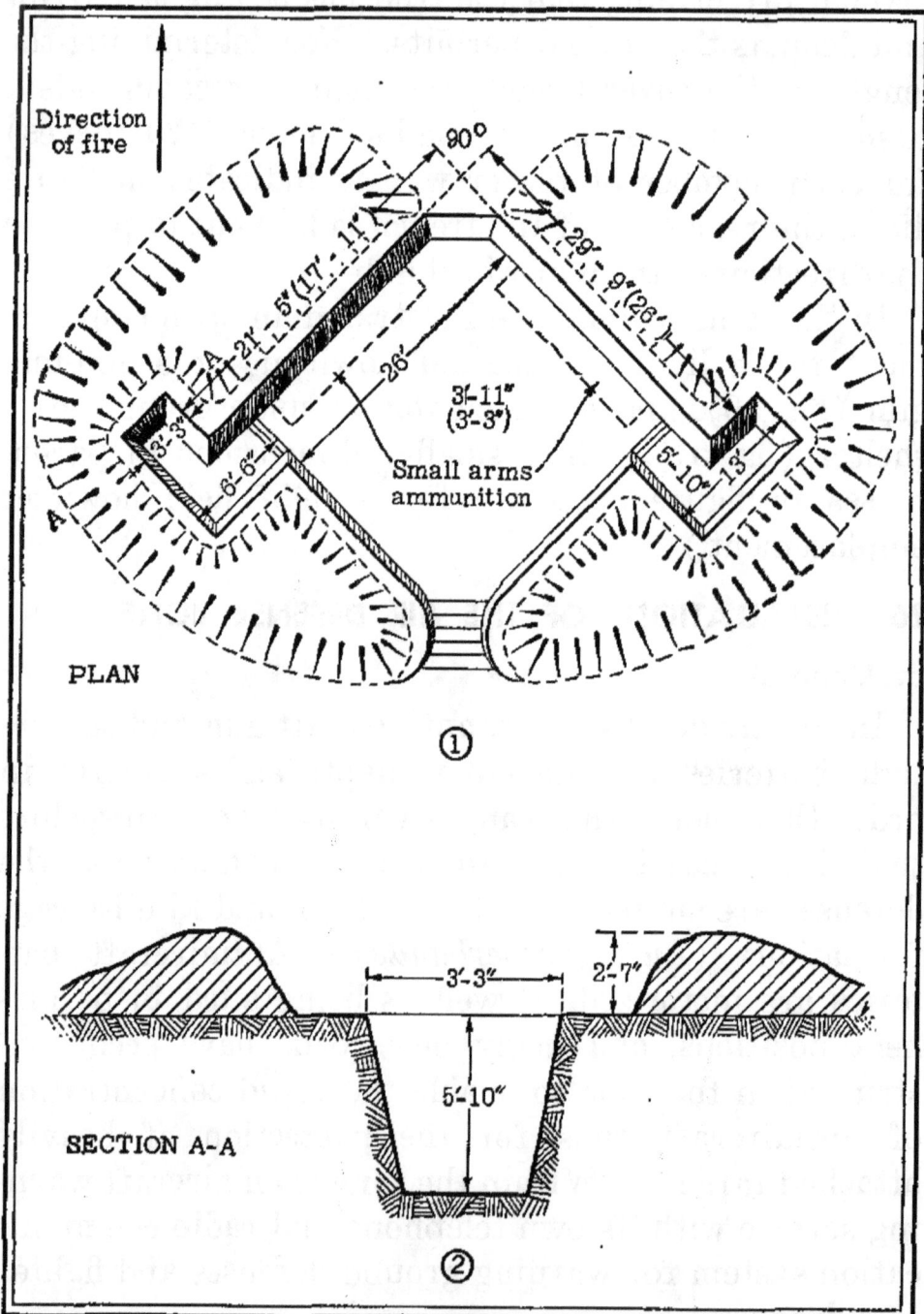

Figure 50.—Open emplacement for light or medium howitzer.

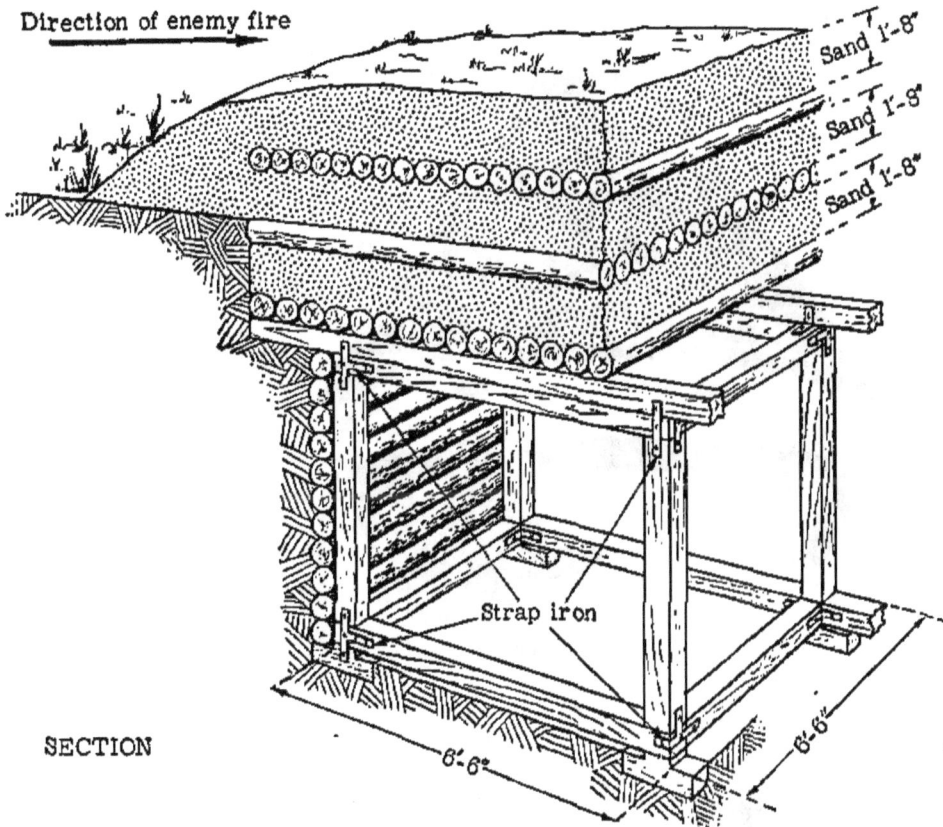

Figure 51.—Shelter for artillery crew.

struction according to the type of equipment and the time, material, and labor that are available. Square, rectangular, and circular emplacements made of earth and sand, or concrete, have been noted in aerial photographs. Depending on the nature of the ground and field-of-fire requirements, the emplacements may be dug into the ground, or installed on the surface, or on raised platforms or towers.

Figure 52 illustrates a type of heavy fortified tower in the air defense zone. The walls, which appear to be about 8 feet thick, contain both fire and observation posts, and antiaircraft weapons or optical instruments may be mounted on the railed platform on the roof.

Figure 52.—Fortified tower in air defense zone.

b. Sandbag Emplacements

The standard sandbag-and-earth emplacement for the 88-mm antiaircraft gun, as described in German manuals, is roughly circular, with a diameter of 24 feet. The emplacement has two entrances, approximately opposite each other, which are about 7 feet wide and are made generally of staggered sandbag walls.

c. Concrete Emplacements

A typical recent type of antiaircraft layout that is frequently observed contains a total of 10 concrete emplacements. In the description given below, the measurements quoted were obtained from photographic interpretations and therefore are subject to a margin of error of 10 to 15 percent:

(1) Six gun emplacements, each 22 feet square, laid out in a rough circle.

(2) Two additional emplacements in the center of the layout, one containing a range finder and measuring 18 feet square, and the other containing the auxiliary predictor and measuring 11 feet by 18 feet. These two emplacements are about 14 feet apart and are connected by a trench.

(3) Two emplacements outside the layout, one containing the fire control station (*Kommandogerät*) and measuring 22 feet square, and the other, octagonal in shape, containing an antiaircraft gun and measuring 22 feet across. The reason for siting this gun emplacement outside the layout is not known.

27. OBSTACLES

a. Antitank Obstacles

Antitank obstacles extend along nearly the entire front of the West Wall. Natural terrain features such as earth folds, dry stream beds, cliffs, and woods have been fully exploited and improved. Such existing natural earthworks as masonry walls, dams, and canals have been strengthened and adapted, and, wherever possible, supplemented by ditches (fig. 53).

When the terrain is such that artificial obstacles are required, a continuous band of dragon's teeth is commonly found (figs. 54, 55, and 56). This obstacle usually consists of four or five rows of reinforced concrete pyramids, cast on a common base in such a way as to stop a tank by "bellying." Figure 56 illustrates a common arrangement of five rows of teeth. It is known that from two to four rows of teeth have been added to the original obstacle in some sectors.

Dragon's teeth are usually sited in a long, generally straight line, and covered by fire from antitank weapons in concrete pillboxes and in open emplacements. Figure 55, however, shows a line that curves with the terrain. The dragon's teeth obstacle is straight rather than zigzag in trace in order that it may be accurately covered by fire of the final protective-line type. The antitank weapons sited behind these obstacles apparently cover a sector of front that is limited by the normal 60° traverse of weapons in embrasures. However, greater flexibility is achieved by emplacing some weapons in the open, and by moving other weapons from one embrasure to another in concrete works, as the situation warrants, in order to obtain wider or different fields of fire.

Other conventional types of artificial tank obstacles occur less frequently in the West Wall. One is a field of posts, tree trunks, or steel rails installed upright in a manner similar to the dragon's teeth. This obstacle

Figure 53.—West Wall antitank ditch.

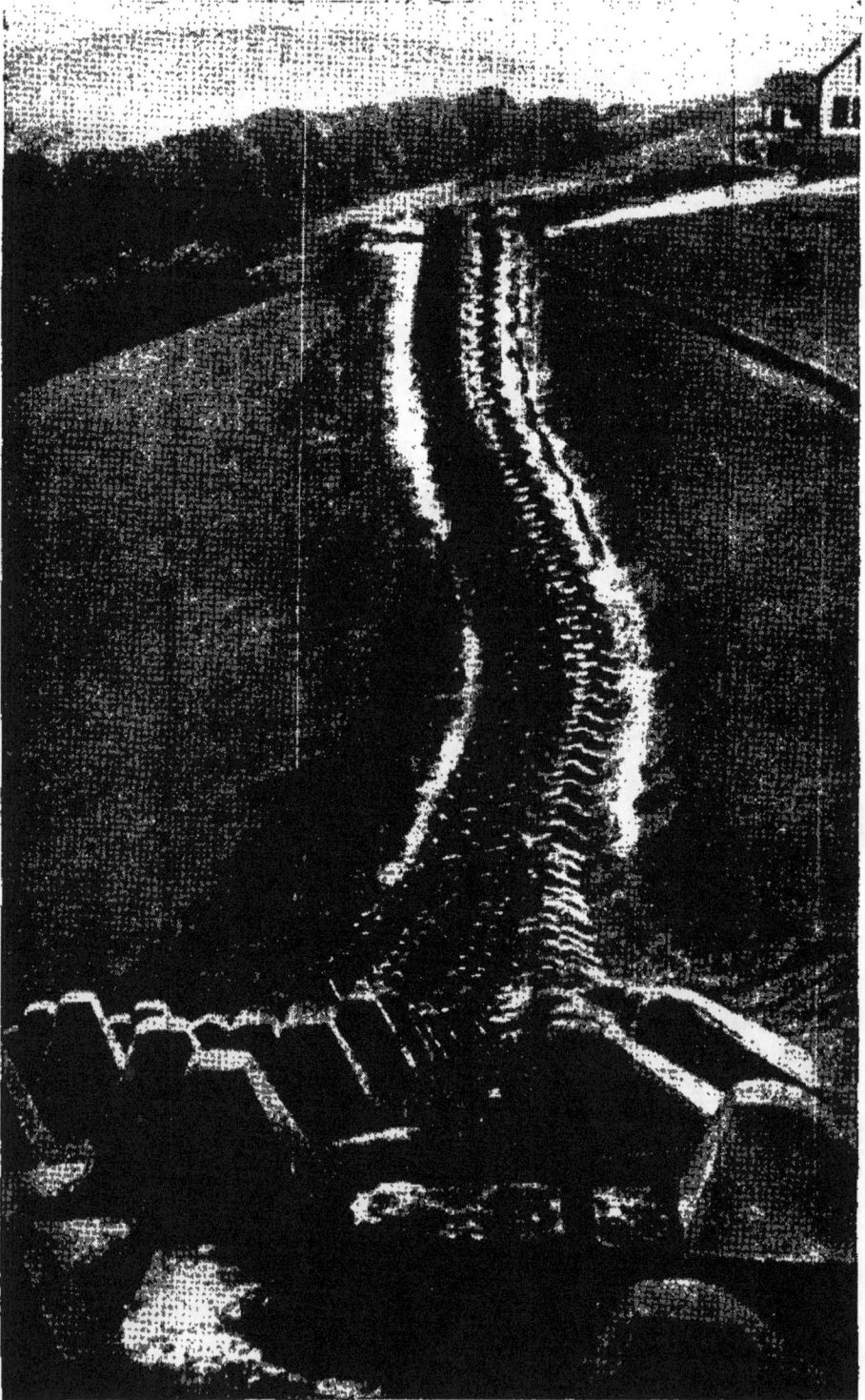

Figure 54.—Drogon's teeth obstacle.

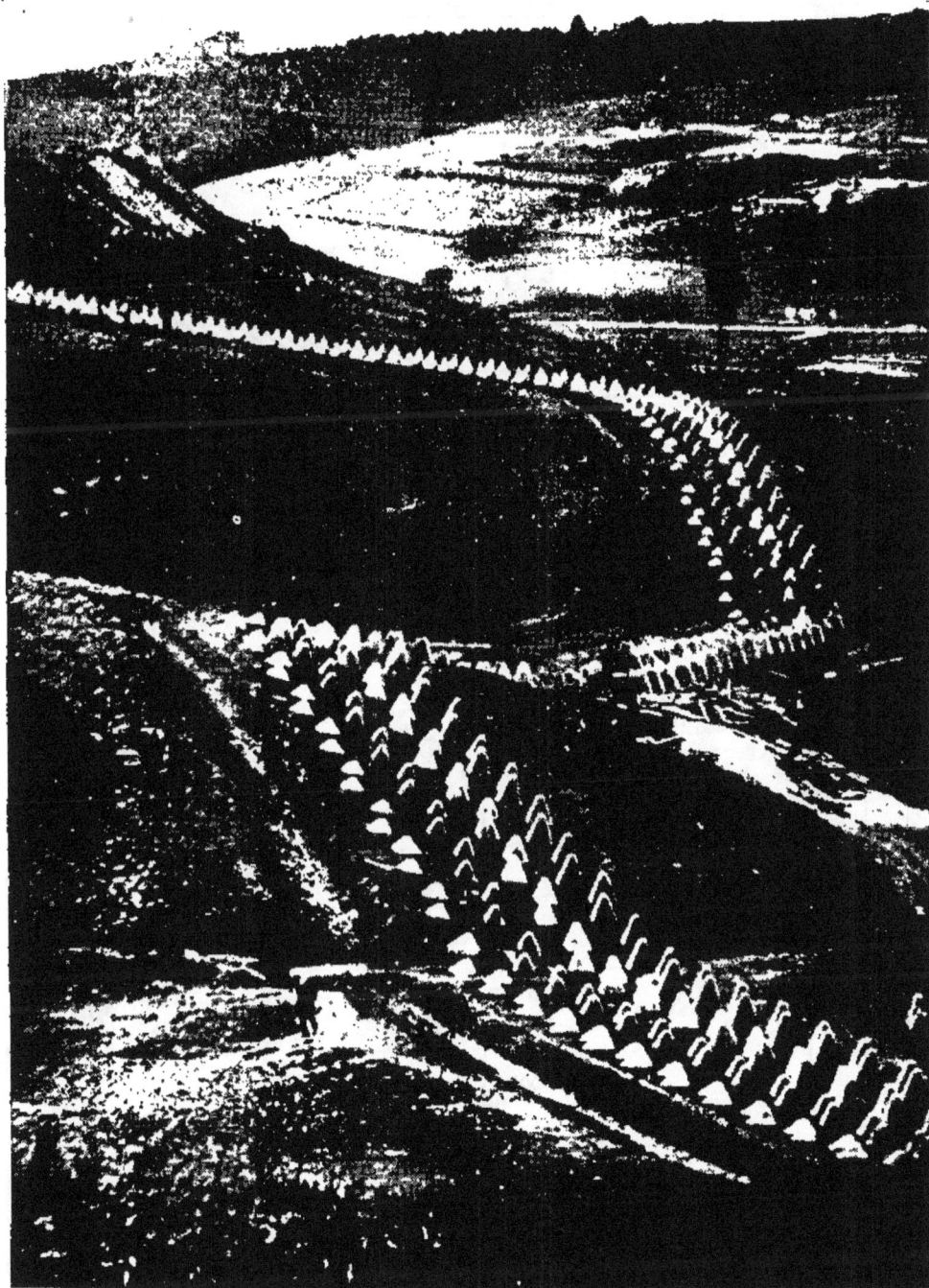

Figure 55.—Dragon's teeth obstacle adapted to broken terrain.

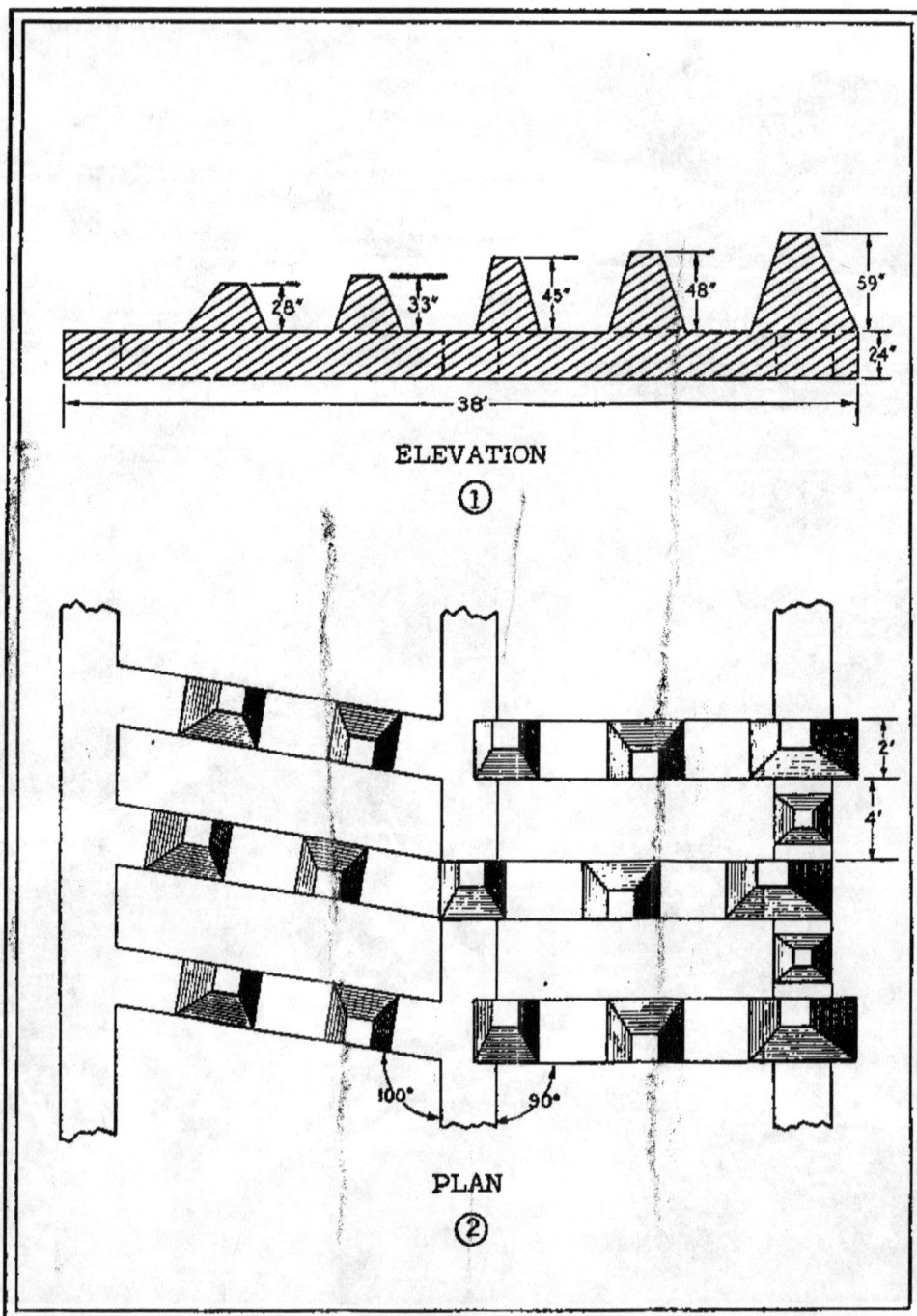

Figure 56.—Typical arrangement of dragon's teeth obstacle.

is the German equivalent of the U. S. "asparagus-bed" obstacle. Another type is the angle-iron grill (fig. 57), which is constructed in heights up to 6 feet. Other obstacles photographed in the West Wall include continuous lines of 6-foot craters, and of angle-iron "hedgehogs," or chevaux-de-frise, about 5 feet high (fig. 58). Where a line of tank obstacles crosses a road, one of numerous types of removable road blocks usually appears. One of the commonest types consists of heavy steel bars that may be placed in slots in reinforced concrete supports (fig. 59) built on opposite sides of a road. Bars of the desired size and number are hoisted into place as needed.

In the approaches to defenses, particularly in avenues of advance favorable for armored forces, antitank ditches and dragon's teeth are usually complemented by deep fields of antitank mines. These fields will be installed by the Germans when their areas of permanent fortifications are threatened. They normally place their mines in rectangular blocks about 30 paces wide by 40 paces deep. The blocks are echeloned with respect to each other so that a field will not be linear in extent. Depth is attained by placing one set of rectangular blocks of mines in rear of another, to the desired total depth of the mine field.

Some of the mines will be booby-trapped to menace personnel who attempt to clear the mine fields. Moreover, antipersonnel mines will be interspersed among antitank mines further to complicate the problem of clearing the fields.

Figure 57.—Angle-iron grill obstacle.

Figure 58.—Cheval-de-frise obstacle.

Figure 59.—Concrete supports for removable road blocks.

b. Personnel Obstacles

Wire entanglements are placed in thick belts 30 to 50 yards wide, between tank obstacles and defending bunkers. Where no tank obstacle exists, wire entanglements are placed within effective machine-gun range. The usual height of wire entanglements is about 3 feet. Often there are two bands of wire, each 30 feet wide and separated by about 30 feet. German fences are densely laced with wire (fig. 60). The Germans normally site their fences in zigzag fashion along the line of final protective fire from machine guns in pillboxes.

In addition to the tactical wire in front of the position, individual pillboxes are surrounded by protective wire at a distance of 25 to 50 yards (fig. 61) in order to prevent assaulting infantry from reaching an easy grenade-throwing range. Antipersonnel devices, including booby traps, are placed within the obstacles to discourage attacking troops in their efforts to effect a breach.

Figure 60.—West Wall barbed-wire obstacle.

Figure 61.—Protective wire around pillbox.

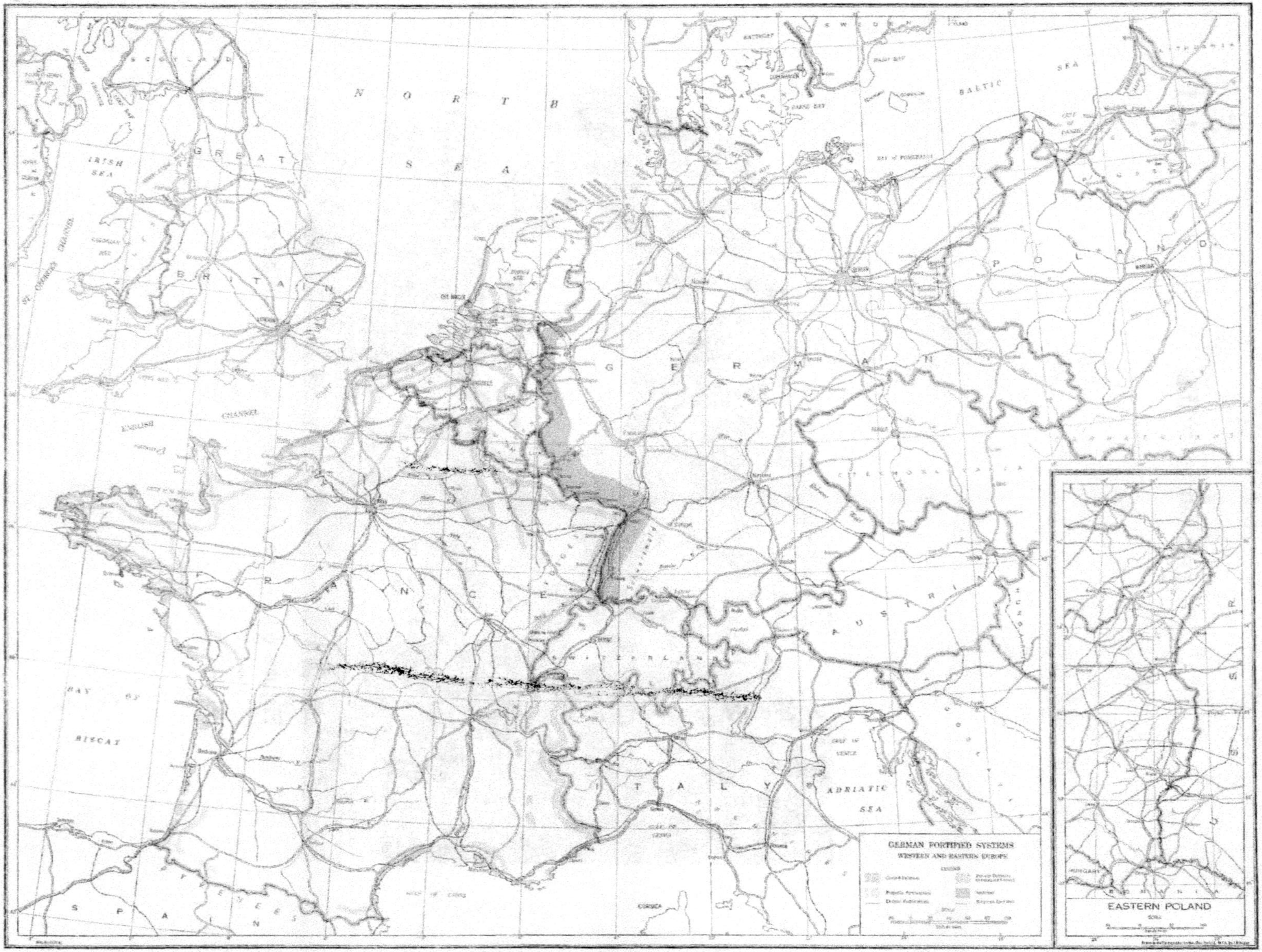

Figure 1.—German fortified systems, western and eastern Europe.

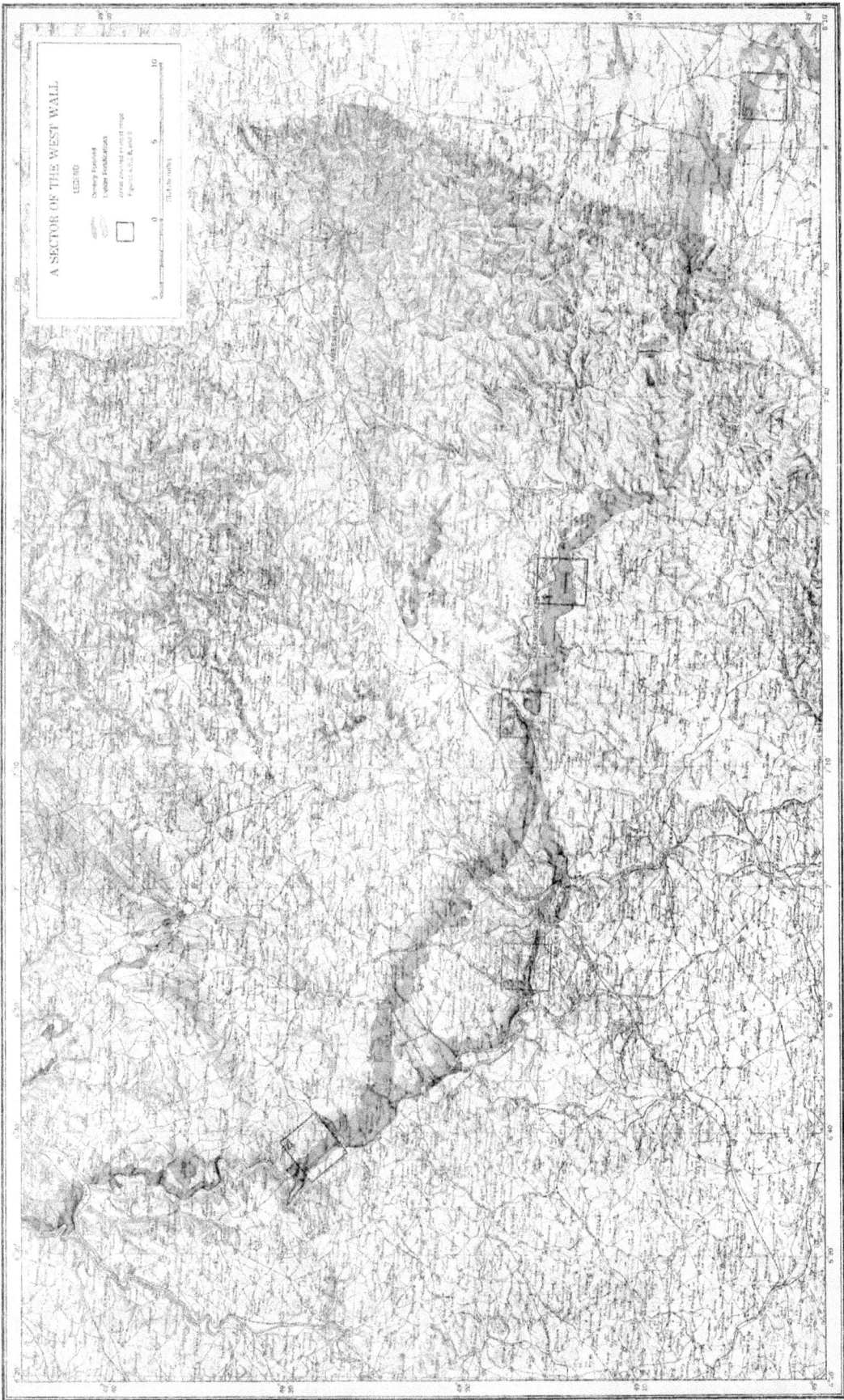

Figure 2.—Map of a sector of the West Wall.

www.ingramcontent.com/pod-product-compliance
Lightning Source LLC
Chambersburg PA
CBHW080511110426
42742CB00017B/3069